FLAGS

THROUGH THE AGES

TASMANIA

SOLOMON
ISLANDS

FIJI
ISLANDS

TERRITORY
OF PAPUA

BRITISH RESIDENT,
GILBERT & ELLIS ISLANDS

WESTERN PACIFIC
HIGH COMMISSIONERS

AFRICA

BRITISH CENTRAL AFRICA

BRITISH EAST AFRICA

SAMOLILAND

UNION OF SOUTH AFRICA

SIERRA LEONE

GOLD COAST

GAMBIA

ST. HELENA

CHINA

NIGERIA

UGANDA

HONG KONG

WEIHAIWEI

EAST INDIES

CEYLON

MAURITIAS

STRAITS SETTLEMENTS

SEYCHELLES

FLAGS
THROUGH THE AGES

A GUIDE TO THE WORLD OF FLAGS, BANNERS, STANDARDS AND ENSIGNS

ALFRED ZNAMIEROWSKI

southwater

This edition is published by Southwater

Southwater is an imprint of
Anness Publishing Limited
Hermes House
88-89 Blackfriars Road
London SE1 8HA
tel. 020 7401 2077
fax 020 7633 9499

Distributed in the USA by
Anness Publishing Inc.
27 West 20th Street
Suite 504
New York NY 10011
tel. 212 807 6739
fax 212 807 6813

Distributed in the UK by
The Manning Partnership
251-253 London Road East
Batheaston
Bath BA1 7RL
tel. 01225 852 727
fax 01225 852 852

Distributed in Australia by
Sandstone Publishing
Unit 1, 360 Norton Street
Leichhardt
New South Wales 2040
tel. 02 9560 7888
fax 02 9560 7488

Publisher: Joanna Lorenz
Project Editor: Helen Marsh
Designer: Michael Morey
Flag artwork: Alfred Znamierowski
Map artwork: Mike Taylor

Previously published as part of a larger compendium, *The World Encyclopedia of Flags*

Author's Acknowledgements

The author wishes to dedicate this book to the memory of his late teacher and friend Dr Ottfried Neubecker,
and to extend thanks for encouragement, help and support to Beata Gierblinska (Warsaw),
Whitney Smith (Winchester, Massachussetts), Roman Klimes (Bonn) and Jacek Skorupski (Warsaw).

Publisher's Acknowledgements

The publisher would like to thank the following for kindly supplying photographs for this book: page 24 *b* Bruno Barbey at Magnum;
page 33 *br* Beata Gierblinska; page 40 *br* Miroslaw Stelmach; page 41 *m* NASA; page 43 *tl* Chad Ehlers and Tony Stone Images,
tr Ron Sherman and Tony Stone Images; page 45 *tr* Ron Sherman and Tony Stone Images; page 47 *m* Raghu Rai and Magnum;
page 50 *b* Hulton Getty; page 97 *b* National Geographic Society.

The publishers would also like to thank: The Flag Design Center, Warsaw for use of images from the archive;
Judy Cox; John Clarke; and Dr Lawrie Wright of Queen Mary and Westfield College, University of London.

◆ **TITLE PAGE**
The distinguishing flag of the joint chiefs of
staff vice-chairman in the United States of
America.

◆ **FRONTISPIECE**
Badges of the British Colonies from *Flags of
Maritime Nations*, 1914..

◆ **HALF TITLE PAGE**
The flag belonging to the President of
Czechoslovakia from 1920-1939 and from
1945-1960.

◆ **OPPOSITE PAGE**
The All-German Olympic flag, used from
1959-1968

CONTENTS

GREAT BRITAIN, ROYAL STANDARD. GREAT BRITAIN, UNION JACK. GREAT BRITAIN, MAN-OF-WAR. ARGENTINE REPUBLIC, WAR.† CUBA LIBRE. AUSTRIA-HUNGARY, IMP. STAR. AUSTRIA-HUNGARY, WAR. AUSTRIA-HUNGARY, MERCHANT. GERMANY, MAN-OF-WAR.

GREAT BRITAIN, NAVAL RESERVE. GREAT BRITAIN, MERCHANT. ALGIERS. BELGIUM, ROYAL STANDARD.* BRAZIL, MERCHANT. BOLIVIA, ENSIGN.* CHILI, NATIONAL STANDARD. GERMANY, MERCHANT. GERMANY, IMPERIAL STANDARD.

CHINA, IMPERIAL STANDARD. CHINA, MERCHANT. COCHIN-CHINA, MERCHANT. MALTA. UNITED STATES, UNION JACK. UNITED STATES, PRESIDENT. UNITED STATES, REAR ADMIRAL. UNITED STATES, SEC. OF NAVY. HAYTI, MAN-OF-WAR.* HONDURAS, ENSIGN. ITALY, ROYAL STANDARD. URUGUAY, ENSIGN.

COREA, ENSIGN. COSTA RICA, MAN-OF-WAR.* ECUADOR, ENSIGN. EGYPT (AND TURKEY), ENSIGN. UNITED STATES, YACHT. UNITED STATES, REVENUE. ITALY, MAN-OF-WAR.† JAPAN, JACK. LIBERIA, ENSIGN. MEXICO, MAN-OF-WAR.*

DENMARK, ROYAL STANDARD. DENMARK, MERCHANT. GREECE, MAN-OF-WAR.† GUATEMALA, ENSIGN. UNITED STATES, QUARANTINE. UNITED STATES, ENSIGN. UNITED STATES, LONG PENNANT. U.S. COMMODORE'S PENNANT. MOROCCO, MERCHANT. NETHERLANDS, ROYAL.* NORWAY, ROYAL. NORWAY, MERCHANT.

NEW ZEALAND, ENSIGN. NICARAGUA, ENSIGN. PARAGUAY, MAN-OF-WAR. PARAGUAY, MERCHANT. PERSIA, ENSIGN. PERU, MAN-OF-WAR.* PORTUGAL, ROYAL STANDARD. PORTUGAL, ENSIGN.* SAN DOMINGO, MAN-OF-WAR.* SAN SALVADOR, MERCHANT. SIAM, ENSIGN. SOCIETY ISLANDS, ENSIGN.

HAWAII, ENSIGN. SWITZERLAND, ENSIGN. SAMOA, MERCHANT. SPAIN, MAN-OF-WAR. FLAGS OF THE COMMERCIAL CODE OF SIGNALS. SPAIN, MERCHANT. SWEDEN, ROYAL STANDARD. SWEDEN, MERCHANT. TRIPOLI, ENSIGN. FLAGS OF THE COMMERCIAL CODE OF SIGNALS. TUNIS, MAN-OF-WAR.* U. S. OF COLOMBIA, ENSIGN. MONTENEGRO, STATE. MONTENEGRO, MARINE.

FRANCE, ENSIGN. VENEZUELA, WAR.* RED CROSS SOCIETY. CANADA. IRELAND. ORANGE FREE STATE. ROUMANIA. CONGO. RUSSIA, MAN-OF-WAR.

BULGARIA, MERCHANT. BURMAH. ZANZIBAR. SCOTLAND. SOUTH AFRICAN REPUBLIC. ARABIA. MADAGASCAR. RUSSIA, MERCHANT. RUSSIA, IMPERIAL STANDARD.

MALTA. 129. | MALTA. 130. | NAPLES, SICILIAN STANDARD. 131. | NAPLES. War and Merchant 132 | NAPOLITAN SIGNAL FOR A PILOT. 133.

IONIAN ISLES. 134. | WALLACHIAN MERCHANT. 135. | OTTOMAN EMPIRE. 136. | THE GRAND SEIGNIOR 137. | GRAND VIZIER. 138.

TURKISH MAN OF WAR. 139. | TURKISH MERCHANT.* † 140. | OTTOMAN GREEK. 141. | GREECE. 142. | GREEK MERCHANT. 143.

NETHERLANDS: STANDARD. 144. | FLAG OF THE NETHERLANDS. 145. | BELGIUM: STANDARD. 146. | BELGIAN MERCHANT. 147. | CITY OF AMSTERDAM. 148.

6

Introduction

The fascinating story of flags is closely interwoven with historical events, reflecting the aspirations and lives of people over many centuries. The eagle-topped standards of the Roman legions, the flame-edged flag of Genghis Khan and the heraldic banners carried by medieval knights in tournament are all part of a continuing development that has led to the flags we know today. Changes in society can be seen in the representations of flags in early maps, books and art, many of which are very decorative. Modern flags show how the revolutions of the 19th century abolished the old order of monarchy, replacing the traditional heraldic flags with simple symbolic designs that carried a very different political and ideological message.

In a useful reference section the physical characteristics of flags are described in detail, followed by the various types of flag, flag usage and etiquette, each with its own separate glossary for ease of reference. A discussion of the flags of emperors, sovereigns and presidents and of government is followed by chapters on military signs from battle banners to war ensigns, including the flags of the armed services. A final, important chapter on flag families shows how the flags of a few countries have influenced those of the rest of the world.

In some flags an emblem such as the Muslim crescent or Scandinavian cross shows that it belongs to a particular "flag family". Kinship within flag families sometimes reaches across the world, indicating that these countries are somehow connected even if physical ties such as colonies no longer exist.

◆ **OPPOSITE ABOVE**
Various types of flags and ensigns as well as royal standards, distinguishing flags, jacks and pennants are represented on this American chart, published by F.E. Wright in 1896.

◆ **OPPOSITE BELOW**
Among flags presented on this plate from Colton's *Delineation of Flags of All Nations* (1862) are royal standards of Naples, the Netherlands and Belgium, the civil ensigns of Turkey and Greece introduced at the end of the 18th century, and the flag of the Ionian Islands under British rule (1817–1864).

The Origin and Development of Flags

*Symbols are sacred things, and one of the chief that every man holds
dear is the national flag. Deep down in our nature is the strong emotion that swells the
heart and brings the tear and makes us follow the flag and die round it rather than let it
fall into the hands of an enemy. This is no new emotion, no growth of a few generations,
but an inheritance from the ages before history began.*

W.J. GORDON, *FLAGS OF THE WORLD*, LONDON, 1915

The origin of flags lies in our remote prehistoric past. When people started to form large groups to live and hunt together, they appointed a leader to rule them and settle disputes. As a mark of office the leader wore a ceremonial head-dress and held a long decorated staff, rod or spear, topped with an ornament or emblem. The staff was also used as a visible sign to rally around, or to point out the direction of a march or attack. This proto-flag is known as a vexilloid.

Later in China, a different tradition developed when silk was invented. This strong, light fabric was ideal for making banners, which were much easier to carry than vexilloids and are easier to see from a distance. From China the use of fabric flags spread to Mongolia, India and Persia, and finally they arrived in Rome and the rest of Europe.

The first vexilloids and flags were military and ceremonial signs. But by the 12th century they began to serve as a way of identifying rulers and their domains, and nationality at sea. During the next two centuries cities and guilds adopted their own flags, and the 17th century saw the introduction of standardized regimental colours, war ensigns, jacks and the house flags of the trading companies. The first national flags on land appeared in the last quarter of the 18th century, as did the flags of yacht clubs. During the 19th and 20th centuries a host of other flags also appeared: flags of government agencies and officials; provincial flags; rank flags in all branches of the armed forces; and flags of schools, universities, scientific institutions, organizations, political parties, trades unions and guerrilla movements. There are also flags of nationalities and ethnic groups, flags of business corporations and sporting clubs, and occasionally flags for fun. It seems that you have no identity unless you have a flag.

♦ **ABOVE**
Standard of West Egypt, found on the sarcophagus of Khons-mose (*c.* 1000 BC).

♦ **ABOVE**
Detail of the palette of Narmer, 3000 BC. The palette is in the Egyptian Museum in Cairo.

♦ **BELOW LEFT**
Detail of the Osiris' misteria stela (2000 BC).

♦ **BELOW**
Standard of the Two Falcons *nome*.

VEXILLOIDS

The original vexilloids were made of wood, feathers and the horns, tails, hooves and skins of animals. Later ornaments or emblems on top of the staff were made of carved and painted wood or metal. We know this from the well-documented Aztec vexilloids, and those of societies that 100 years ago still lived in Stone Age conditions. The characteristic feature of the Aztec vexilloids was extensive use of green quetzal feathers, metals such as gold, silver and copper, and precious stones. The vexilloids still used today by tribes in New Guinea are ancient Melanesian; the way they are made and their symbolism reveal no influence from other cultures. They consist mostly of wood, dried grass and feathers, with emblems of painted wood, feathers and pieces of cloth.

The oldest known vexilloids appear on Egyptian pottery of the Gerzean period (3400 BC) and on the reverse of the King Narmer palette (3000 BC). They were the signs of *nomes*, the provinces of pre-dynastic Egypt. The *nomes* were named after things or animals (Two Falcons, Sceptre, Ibis, Double Feather, and so on), which were depicted as highly stylized emblems on the vexilloids. Some provincial vexilloids displayed the emblems of local gods. They were made of wood, and the emblems were painted.

There is very little evidence of Assyrian, Babylonian and Persian vexilloids, although the oldest vexilloid still in existence was carried in Persia 5000 years ago. It has a metal staff, with a finial in the form of an eagle, and a square metal "flag" covered with reliefs. Two primitive vexilloids appear on a stela of Naramsin, King of Babylonia (*c.*3000 BC). At Alacahöyük, in north-central Turkey, archaeologists have found Hittite standards dating from *c.*2400–2200 BC. The metal emblems show a stag, a stag with two bulls and a sun disc.

The Romans copied the use of vexilloids as well as the eagle emblem from Persia. The military standard (*signum*) of the Roman legions consisted of a lance with a silver-plated shaft, topped with a crosspiece carrying figures of various beasts. The most important was an eagle

◆ **ABOVE**
Standard of the Double Feather *nome*.

◆ **ABOVE**
Dragon standard from *Psalterium Aureum* (9th century).

◆ **BELOW**
Vexilloids: *(left to right)* Assyrian, Roman, Aztec, Mongolian, Japanese.

(*aquila*). Attached to the shaft were several metal rings in the form of a laurel wreath, and medallions with the eagle of Jupiter or with portraits of the emperor and members of the imperial house. According to Pliny the Elder:

> *Gaius Marius in his second consulship (103 BC) assigned the eagle exclusively to the Roman legions. Before that period it had only held the first rank, there being four others as well – the wolf, the minotaur, the horse and the wild boar – each of which preceded a single division.*

Popular in the Roman Army from the 2nd century was the *draco* (dragon flag), borrowed from the Parthians or Sarmatians, who used this kind of flag several centuries earlier. A hollow bronze dragon's head sat at the top of the staff with a serpent-shaped silk windsock attached. When the wind blew it moved like a serpent and a device in its head made a whistling noise.

The dragon flag was used in Britain during the Dark Ages, and in the 6th century was adopted by the Saxon conquerors. It was borne in front of the armies of the Anglo-Saxons and Normans at least until the 12th century.

The Mongols also had an instantly recognizable vexilloid consisting of a staff topped with a metal ball or spear, with a horse's tail attached to it. These spread quickly among the Turkish people; in the Turkish Army they became the sign of a commander and in the 17th and 18th centuries they were carried before the commanders-in-chief of the Polish Army.

EARLY FLAGS

Long before flags appeared in Europe they had been used in China. Written sources even mention the flag of the Yellow Emperor, a mythological ancestor of the Chinese. The oldest iconographic information on the shape and function of flags in China dates from about 1500 BC. A bamboo staff was topped with a metal trident, to which were attached small rings holding tassels made of horses' tails. The number of narrow ribbons attached to the outer edge denoted the social rank of the flag-bearer, ranging from twelve for the Emperor down to just one for a functionary of the lowest rank. A long, wide, swallow-tailed ribbon was attached to make it into a signal for battle.

The Chinese, who first made cloth out of silk, were the first to make flags out of fabric and attach them sideways to the staff to form a banner. The hierarchy of Chinese society was reflected in a large number of different types of flag for use by the emperor, nobility, commanders of the imperial army, and governors of the provinces and counties. The most common flag symbols were a dragon, tiger, hawk, turtle and snake. The emperor had five chariots, each flying a different flag in yellow, blue, red, white and black. In the course of history the shape of Chinese flags changed to square or triangular with "flammules" (flame-shaped edges), but the hierarchy reflected in the number of flags was maintained. For example, in the 19th century there were nine classes of mandarins and the army used some 50 different flags; there were also special flags for eleven ranks of envoys.

After the Mongols under Kublai Khan conquered China in 1279 they also began to use triangular flags with flammules, mounted sideways on a staff that was topped with the Chinese trident. The Mongols added flames to the trident and attached horses' tails to its base. This was the shape of the flag of Genghis Khan, which carried an image of a gerfalcon (gyrfalcon) and had nine yaks' tails attached to the nine flammules.

The earliest accounts of a flag in Europe are those of Greek writers, who mention a purple flag as the sign of the admiral's ship in the Athenian navy at the end of the 5th century BC. Two Samnite flags from 330 BC appear on frescoes from Paestum (now in the National Museum in Naples), which are the oldest known illustrations of flags in Europe. In the same museum there is a huge mosaic from Pompeii, depicting Alexander the Great defeating the Persians. It shows a Persian standard, an almost square piece of cloth hanging from a crossbar fastened underneath the spear-top of the lance; the bottom edge of the cloth is fringed. According to sketches made when the mosaic was discovered in 1831, the red field carried an image of a golden cock, the Zoroastrian symbol known as *parodash*.

A flag of exactly the same shape and mounted on the staff in the same way was adopted by the Romans for their cavalry and named *vexillum*.

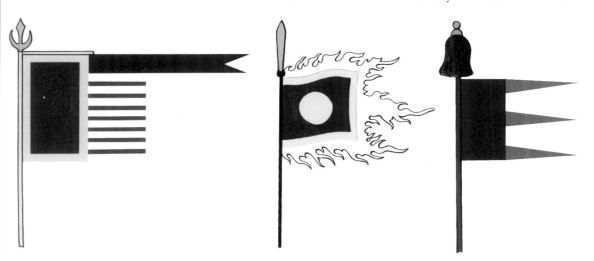

◆ **FAR LEFT**
Reconstruction of the earliest Chinese banner.

◆ **CENTRE LEFT**
Flag of Kublai Khan's armada, (13th century).

◆ **LEFT**
Mongol banner (c.1310).

◆ RIGHT AND FAR RIGHT
Samnite flags on frescoes
from Paestum, 330 BC, are
the oldest flags in Europe
known to date.

The cloth was red, sometimes carrying the name
of the unit, an emblem or a portrait of the
emperor. There was a heavy fringe on the
bottom edge, and the cloth was fastened so that
it always looked draped.

Another similar flag was the *labarum* adopted
by Constantine the Great after his victory over
his rival Maxentius in AD 312, won in the name
of the Christian cross. The purple cloth carried
the gold monogram of Christ, formed of the

◆ RIGHT
Roman vexillum. Bas-relief
from Hadrian's temple in
Rome (AD 145).

first two letters of the Greek word for Christ,
ΧΡΙΣΤΟΣ. The shaft was encased in beaten
gold, and bore medallions with the portraits
of Constantine and his two sons. It seems that
there were two forms of *labarum*; the other one
displayed Christ's monogram at the top of the
staff and the portraits appeared on the cloth.

In the 6th century the Byzantine army
replaced the Roman *vexillum* with a square or
rectangular banner, with one or two triangular
tongues extending from the top edge. In the
8th century they spread to Hungary and Central
Europe. Also in the 8th century the Arabs began
to use triangular flags that were plain black or
white. Later they increased the range of colours
and the flags carried religious inscriptions and
geometric ornaments (because of the religious
ban on representational art).

One of the oldest flags in Europe was not
a flag at all. It was the blue cape of St Martin,
found in his grave by Clovis I of France (who
reigned AD 481–511) and adopted as his banner.
It was later carried in battle by French kings.
In peacetime the cape was kept in a specially
built oratory, which became known as a "chapel"
(from the Latin word *cappa*). Another non-flag
was the royal standard of the Persians, which
for several hundred years until the Muslim
conquest in the 7th century was a blacksmith's
leather apron.

The very beginning of the 9th century saw
the introduction of a new form of flag, the
gonfanon. It is first seen in a mosaic that Pope

Leo III (AD c.750–816) had placed in the Triclinium of the Lateran Palace in Rome in about AD 800. On the right-hand side the mosaic shows Christ handing the keys of the Church to Pope Sylvester and a flag to Constantine, while on the left St Peter presents a cloak to Pope Leo and a flag to Charlemagne. The mosaic commemorates the crowning of Charlemagne as emperor, when he received from the Patriarch of Jerusalem the keys of that city and a flag. The original mosaic has not survived but contemporary sources tell us that the green field of the gonfanon was sprinkled with gold and bore six concentric rings of red, black and gold. This event started a tradition of ceremonial presentations of flags by ecclesiastical authorities to rulers or leaders of expeditions approved by the Church. Emperors also ceremonially handed flags to their subjects. The

◆ **ABOVE**
Labarum of Constantine the Great.

form of the gonfanon was for several centuries reserved for rulers, but after the 11th century it prevailed in the army and from the 12th to the 14th centuries was used by cities.

From the late 8th century, northern European waters were the realm of the Vikings, whose longships sailed as far as Greenland and North America. They raided coastal towns and villages in Britain and France, sometimes settling and intermarrying with the local people. They were the first Europeans to use flags at sea, mounted on vertical staffs. The flags were triangular, with a slightly rounded outer edge; those mounted on the high bows of ships were probably vanes. A gilded vane dating from the 11th century, in the Historiska Museet in Stockholm, has several holes along the curved edge to which rings with tassels could be attached to make the exact shape of the Viking flag. The Vikings had various flags, but the most important seems to have been the raven flag. Both the flag and the raven on its own also appear on Northumbrian coins of the first half of the 10th century.

The Bayeux Tapestry, made in about 1077, contains more than 70 embroidered scenes of the Norman Conquest of England in 1066. It illustrates a very similar flag to the Viking flag, carried immediately behind the Duke of Normandy, William the Conqueror and shows that by that time flags were already being made of cloth. Among the many banners depicted, most of the Norman ones bear a cross, which in pre-heraldic times was the main emblem used by both the military and seamen. More banners with the sign of the cross appeared during the First Crusade (1096–9). One is shown on the seal of Bohemund III, Prince of Antioch. The oldest known account of flags with crosses, the *Gesta Regis Henrici Secundi* by Benedict Abbas, tells us that on 13 January 1188 the Kings of England and France (together with their men) received a white and red cross respectively, while the Count of Flanders received a green cross. We do not know whether these banners were used exclusively on land or also at sea.

EARLY EUROPEAN FLAGS

PENNANT FROM AN IVORY PANEL MADE IN THE CIRCLE OF CHARLES THE BALD (AD c.840).

GONFANON FROM THE WESTMINSTER PSALTER (12TH CENTURY).

PENNANT FROM THE BAYEAUX TAPESTRY (AD c.1077).

GONFANON OF THE MILITIA OF VERONA (12TH CENTURY).

From the 9th to the 12th centuries merchant ships on the North Sea and the Baltic Sea carried a metal gridcross, a symbol of the king's protection, at the top of the mast. From at least the 12th century the same symbol, in the form of a staff topped with a cross, was used on land, mainly by princes and cities in the territories dependent on the German Empire. A second symbol of the king's protection also appeared in the 12th century: a gonfanon without any emblems, attached to a spear or to a staff topped with a cross. This is the *vexillo roseum imperiali* or the *Blutbanner* (blood banner), a red banner presented by the emperor to princes and counts. The *Blutbanner* gave them the right of judicial power over life and death in their domains, and imposed the obligation to contribute men for the imperial army. The *Blutbanner* was awarded also to the cities that became free imperial cities in the 12th and 13th centuries, and to the freed peasants of Schwyz in 1240.

At the beginning of the 13th century merchant ships in northern Europe began to fasten single-coloured gonfanons to the mast, topped with a cross. Those of the Hanseatic cities and of Denmark were red; the English gonfanon was presumably white, later to carry the red cross of St George. In the second half of the 13th century port cities began to differentiate their flags either by dividing them into different coloured areas or by adding simple emblems, the most common of which was the Christian cross. New flags in banner form were placed at the stern, while the mast still carried the single-coloured gonfanons, later replaced by pennants or banners. The oldest is the plain red flag of Hamburg; the date of its adoption is not known, but it was in use from at least the middle of the 13th century. A little later Riga and Lübeck adopted their flags, followed by Stralsund, Elbing, Danzig, Bremen and Rostock in the 14th century, and Königsberg, Wismar and Stettin in the 15th century.

The oldest flag on record in the Mediterranean region is that of Genoa; the earliest illustration, dated 1113, shows it as

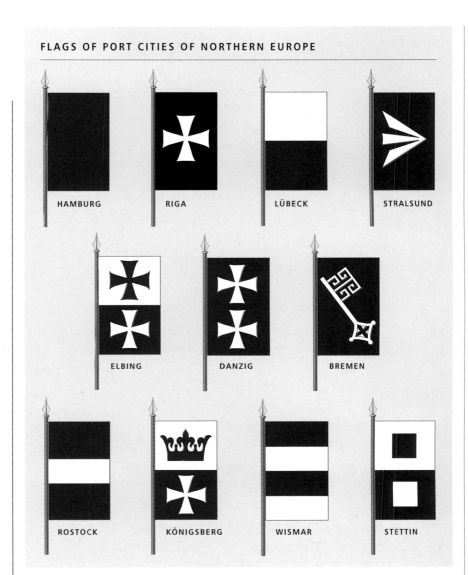

FLAGS OF PORT CITIES OF NORTHERN EUROPE

HAMBURG   RIGA   LÜBECK   STRALSUND

ELBING   DANZIG   BREMEN

ROSTOCK   KÖNIGSBERG   WISMAR   STETTIN

◆ **ABOVE**
Raven flag
(9th century).

white with a red cross. Pisa received the red imperial banner in 1162. Both flags are much older than those of England or Hamburg, which they resemble. Even in the 13th century, when all of these flags were in existence, merchant vessels did not travel very long distances so it was impossible for an English ship to meet a vessel from Genoa or a vessel from Pisa to meet a ship from Hamburg, so the flags could not be confused. Nevertheless Pisa later added a distinctive white cross to its red flag, and the red flag of Hamburg was given a white shield with a red castle (since 1751 the white castle has been located directly on the red background).

In the 14th century the flags of Savoy and Denmark were also identical, but the Danish ships did not venture as far as the Mediterranean. When, 400 years later, they did sail there they adopted especially for that purpose the Danish merchant flag, which had a white square in the centre carrying the royal cipher.

THE AGE OF CHIVALRY

The invention of a helmet to cover and protect the face of a warrior, and thus hide his identity, was one reason why it became necessary to develop signs of identification. The other reason was the widespread use of the cross by all armed forces in Western Europe. The similarity between the banners of friend and foe could cause major misunderstandings on the battlefield.

The basic rules of heraldry were adopted during the Second Crusade (1147–9) and the returning knights took them back to their countries. In the Middle East they had seen the traditional stylization of natural and mythological beasts, and they decided that simple figures on contrasting backgrounds would make excellent signs of identification. The shield was the ideal background. The number of heraldic tinctures was limited to seven: five colours (red, blue, green, black and purple) and two metals (gold and silver). To achieve the best possible identification from a distance the rule of alternation was adopted, which forbade putting colour on colour or metal on metal. A "fimbriation", or border, of metal was used to separate adjacent areas of two colours. The only pre-heraldic device incorporated into the arms was the Christian cross, and to distinguish the crosses that appeared in many arms a great number of different shapes were invented. Other popular heraldic emblems included the lion, eagle, griffin, horse, fleur-de-lis, rose and various weapons.

The invention of heraldry not only helped to distinguish flags denoting ducal, princely or civic domains, but also led to a rapid growth in personal flags. As well as a coat of arms, each qualified person carried an armorial banner, which now became the principal kind of flag. It was either square or much wider than it was long, and sizes varied according to the rank of its owner. According to one medieval source, the banner of an emperor should be 1.8 m (2 yd) square, that of a king 1.5 m (5 ft) square, that of a prince or duke 1.2 m (4 ft) square, and that of an earl, marquis, viscount or baron 90 cm (3 ft) square.

The personal heraldic badges of rulers, unrelated to their coats of arms, appeared on their standards, banners and the flags of their retainers. The most famous ones still remembered are the white and red roses of York and Lancaster, the white boar of Richard III, the salamander of Francis I, the porcupine of Louis XII and the radiant sun of Louis XIV.

A distinct type of armorial flag, designed to indicate the rallying point or headquarters of the arms-bearer, or "armiger", was the standard. It was a long, tapering flag with a rounded swallow-tail, and it bore the livery colours arranged horizontally. The hoist carried either the national mark (for example, the cross of St George, the cross of St Andrew or the cross of Burgundy) or a coat of arms in the form of an armorial banner. Next appeared the heraldic badge of the arms-bearer with his motto, and then another badge or crest, and around the edge was a border of pieces in the livery colour.

◆ BELOW
Banners of Swiss troops, 15th century.

CIVIC BANNERS IN THE 14TH CENTURY

STRASBOURG FLORENCE COLOGNE

Only the arms-bearer could carry his banner or standard, so three other types of flag were used by his retainers: the guidon, pennon and badge-flag. The guidon was a simpler version of the standard. It was also tapered but was shorter with a descate outer edge (see *Flag Design*), bore the national device on the inner edge and had one badge on the livery colours. It was used on horseback, and was a precursor of the cavalry guidon. The pennon was a swallow-tailed flag carried on a mounted warrior's lance. In most cases it bore the badge on a background in the livery colours. The badge-flag was a rectangular flag with the background divided in the livery colours, bearing the heraldic badge or badges.

From the beginning of the heraldic period arms were also adopted and used by ecclesiastics and military orders such as the Knights Templar, the Knights of St John of Jerusalem, great Spanish and Portuguese orders and the Teutonic Knights. The arms and armorial banners of bishops and the abbots of monasteries did not represent them but the orders they temporarily represented; they were also signs of their domains. The rise of the guilds and universities also contributed to the increase in the use of arms and armorial banners as they began to

obtain charters from the crown and were granted arms. An even greater impact was created by the steady growth in the number of towns that adopted arms. Civic armorial banners became the real national flags for the burghers, as the symbols of their rights and privileges.

Not all banners in the Age of Chivalry were armorial. There was also extensive use of Christian symbols in non-heraldic form, including representations of the Holy Trinity, the Holy Ghost, the vernicle (veronica) and scenes of the Crucifixion. As well as banners with symbols of the saints, such as the cross of St George or the lion of St Mark, there were banners displaying the painted figures of saints with their attributes. The most popular were St Peter with his keys, St Andrew with a diagonal cross, St George (mounted) slaying the dragon, St Michael overcoming the Devil, St Paul with a book and sword, and St Catherine with the wheel. The lion of St Mark became the emblem of the Republic of Venice in the pre-heraldic period, the eagle of St John was adopted by the monarchs of Spain, St Peter's keys became the emblem of the papacy, and St Andrew's cross was adopted as the national symbol of Scotland and, in a slightly different form, by Burgundy and later by Spain. Banners with the figures of saints or the Virgin Mary were used until the 17th century as military signs, and also as the ceremonial banners of towns.

◆ **FAR RIGHT**
Italian *portolano*, 1544.

Even before the heraldic age, as early as the 11th century, peculiar vehicles called *carroccio* appeared in northern Italy which were designed to carry huge civic flags. In France *carrocci* appeared a century later, and German versions by the 13th century. They were the centre of all civic festivities and served as a rallying point during battle. The most ceremonial were made of fine wood, inlaid with gold, silver and ivory. According to the *Chronicle of Charlemagne* in the late 9th century, the Saracens used a *carroccio* "which eight oxen bore, upon which their red flag was elevated". From other sources we know that a *carroccio* appeared on the battlefield at the Battle of the Standard near Northallerton, Yorkshire, in 1138: indeed, the battle was named after it. In this the English displayed not only the banners of their patron saints, but also the consecrated Host. In 1191, during a battle with the Saracens near Acre, the banner of Richard I was flown from a *carroccio*. An eye-witness described the vehicle:

It consists, then, of a very long beam, like the mast of a ship, placed upon four wheels in a frame very solidly fastened together and bound with iron, so that it seems incapable of yielding either to sword, axe or fire. Affixed to the very top of this, the royal flag, commonly called banner, flies in the wind.

He explains that "because it stands fast as a sign to all the people, it is called the Standard". In the Battle of Bouvines in 1214 the *carroccio* of Emperor Otto IV was topped by a golden eagle. In the 12th and 13th centuries *carrocci* were in general use in the armies of western Europe and the transference of its original Italian name was completed in the 13th century.

Displays of banners were not limited to the battlefield. Tournaments were enormously popular from the 13th to the 16th centuries. Announced by heralds in many countries, they were an opportunity for knights from all parts of Europe to meet and exhibit their proficiency in handling a horse and weapons. During the

tournament the heralds presented the personal coats of arms of the participants.

The main sources of information about medieval flags are coins and medals, grants of arms, illustrations in chronicles, mosaics and paintings in numerous churches. Especially valuable are some of the armorial rolls. The oldest is the *Zürcher Wappenrolle* (1340), which presents 28 flags of German, Austrian and Bohemian cities and bishoprics; the flags of Strasbourg and Cologne illustrated are taken from this document. The flag of Florence is taken from illustrations in the *Cronaca del Sercambi* (end of the 14th century).

Important information about flags used at sea from the 14th to the 16th centuries can be gleaned from *portolanos*. These are navigational charts depicting coastlines and ports, some rivers and mountain ranges, and flags and coats of arms. Often the flags are very small and their design simplified, but the *portolanos* still contain valuable data. These and the manuscript of a Franciscan friar, a native of Spain, are the oldest sources depicting the flags of North Africa and the Middle East. The manuscript, written and illuminated in about 1350, has a long Spanish title that translates into English as the *Book of the Knowledge of All the Kingdoms, Countries, and Lordships that there are in the World and of the Ensigns and Arms of Each Country and Lordship; also of the Kings and Lords Who Govern Them.* Although the friar claimed to have visited all the places he described, from Spain to China and

◆ **ABOVE LEFT**
Banner of Brandenburg, wood engraving from the *Arms Book of Master IK*, 16th century.

◆ **ABOVE RIGHT**
Banner of Chur, wood engraving by Conrad Schmidt, first half of the 16th century.

◆ **ABOVE**
Banner of Brandenburg from *Banderia Prutenorum*, 1448.

EARLY JAPANESE FLAGS

SASHIMONO

TWO VARIATIONS
OF NOBORI

from Norway to Egypt, some of his accounts are not very reliable; nevertheless the text has great value as the earliest account of flags of all nations, with illustrations of nearly 100 flags.

The first authoritative vexillological work was by the Polish historian Jan Dlugosz in 1448. Entitled *Banderia Prutenorum*, it contains detailed descriptions and measurements, as well as large and exact colour illustrations, of all 56 banners captured by the Polish-Lithuanian troops at Tannenberg in 1410.

From the end of the 15th century, banners were often depicted on stained-glass panels, mainly the Swiss *Standesscheiben*. In later centuries woodcarvings in numerous books show banner-bearers with banners of various domains and cities. Especially valuable are a print with representations of the Julius Banners, published in 1513 in Zürich; the *Arms Book of Master IK* (1545), with 144 banners of the cities and territories of the Holy Roman Empire; and the woodcarvings of Conrad Schmidt.

Although the use of symbols was universal among civilized communities, it is only in Europe and Japan that comprehensive heraldic systems developed. The Japanese *mons* are the equivalent of the heraldic badge rather than the heraldic figure. They do not appear on a shield, but in other respects they play the same role as the arms in Europe. The *mon* is a hereditary symbol, and since the 17th century there has been a legal requirement of registration. Like arms, the *mon* is used on banners, armour and the clothes of the retainers of great lords. It decorates castles, carriages, lanterns and the belongings of the individual and his family. *Mons* are usually symmetrical, simple and stylized representations of flowers (mallow, apricot, wisteria), birds (crane, wild goose) or everyday objects (fan, arrow, hatchet) or geometric designs. The banners used in Japan since the Middle Ages differed from both the Chinese and European ones. They were attached to the staff in the same way as Chinese banners but the shape of the cloth was different, the width being several times greater than the length. The *mon* was often repeated several times on the banner. These banners, like the much smaller *sashimono* banners, were fastened into a socket attached to the back of a cuirass, a piece of chest armour. Modern Japanese banners are rectangular, with the *mon* in the centre. Recently the *mons* have come to represent not only families but also cities and provinces.

◆ **RIGHT**
Mons appear on flags of all Japanese and noble families, as we see on this plate from *Herold*, 1909.

MODERN FLAGS

In the 16th century the general use of armorial banners ended. Although the monarchs of a few countries such as Great Britain retained their armorial banners, most of the royal flags displayed at sea after this date were single-coloured and bore the whole achievement of arms, i.e. with helmets, mantlings, crests, supporters, collars of orders and mottoes.

The first modern flag was the Dutch revolutionary *Prinsenvlag*, composed of simple stripes instead of heraldic devices, followed by the flags created after the revolutions in America and France. The design of these newly created flags reflected the idea that, with the abolition of monarchy, the heraldic system of identification was also rejected. The colours and designs acquired symbolic meaning and flags began to carry ideological and political messages. Flags were based on simple shapes and in most cases only very simple emblems were used. The most popular emblem was the five-pointed star, a symbol of liberty and independence.

This trend has survived to the present day. Even when thousands and even tens of thousands of flags exist at the same time, it is possible to create quite simple yet very distinctive designs. Some recent, but now obsolete, flags are illustrated below. At the time that the Chinese flag was adopted, consisting only of simple stripes, there were many other striped flags, especially in Europe. Nevertheless, since they were bicolours or tricolours, the Chinese flag with its five colours was still very distinctive. The flag of Malaya had different colours and bore the tiger badge. The flag of Manchukuo displayed the same colours as the earlier Chinese flag, but because of the canton it was distinctively different. The thin stripes in the flag of South Vietnam were the only device of this kind among all the world's flags, and the emblems on the flags of Lesotho and Surinam were also very distinctive. The flag of Congo for most of the time was the only flag to display a large star in its centre.

The best insight into the development of modern flags is provided by numerous charts and albums. The first collections of flags used at sea are in Dutch manuscripts of 1667 and 1669, and in a manuscript from 1670 ascribed to J. Moutton of France. The first English collections of flags for use at sea appeared in the notebook of William Downman (1685) and in *Insignia Navalia*, a manuscript by Lieutenant John Graydon dated 1686. The most thorough flag book of this period was *Nieuwe Hollandse Scheeps-bouw* by Carl Allard, published in Amsterdam in 1694 and reprinted several times; it was also extensively copied by other authors. The best were Cornelius Dankerts, who produced the first flag chart *c.*1700 entitled

MODERN FLAGS

CHINA (1912–1923)

FEDERATED MALAY STATES (1905–1948)

MANCHUKUO (1932–1945)

SOUTH VIETNAM (1948–1975)

BELGIAN CONGO (1885–1960)

SURINAM (1959–1975)

LESOTHO (1966–1987)

RHODESIA (1968–1979)

TABLE DES PAVILLONS QUIL'ON ARBORE *Dans toute les Parties du Monde Connu. Conservant la Marinne.*

NIEUWE TAFEL VAN AL DE ZEE. Vaarende **VLAGGE des Weerelts.** tot Amsterdam By **CORNELIS DANCKERTS**

PAVILLON DE St. GEORGE PAVILLON de l'ISLE de MAN

PAVILLON DES INDES ORIENTALES D'ECOSSE PAVILLON de DIVISION des VAISSEAUX ECOSSOIS

◆ **ABOVE**
Dutch flag chart by
C. Dankerts (c.1700).

◆ **RIGHT**
Page from the book by
Jaques van den Kiebom,
*La Connaissance des Pavillons
ou Bannières, que la Plûspart
des Nations Arborent en
Mer*, 1737.

Table des Pavillons quil'on arbore dans toute les Parties du Monde Connu, Consernant la Marinne, and Jaques van den Kiebom, who in 1737 published the book *La Connaissance des Pavillons ou Bannières, que la Plûspart des Nations Arborent en Mer.* In the 19th century most charts were folded in handbooks. The best are *Plates Descriptive of the Maritime Flags of all Nations,* published by J.W. Norie in 1819, and *Three Hundred and Six Illustrations of the Maritime Flags of all Nations,* originally compiled by J.W. Norie and considerably augmented by J.S. Hobbs in 1848. The first official handbook on flags was compiled by Captain Le Gras and published in 1858 by the Secretary of State for the French Imperial Navy under the title *Album des Pavillons, Guidons, Flammes, de toutes les*

◆ **LEFT**
A fragment of the French flag chart from *Tableau des Pavillons que la Plûspart des Nations Arborent à la Mer*, 1756.

Puissances Maritimes. Ten years later the American Bureau of Navigation published the album *Flags of Maritime Nations from the Most Authentic Sources.* In 1874 George Hounsell with the approval of the British Admiralty produced *Flags and Signals of All Nations*, and in 1905 the German Admiralty followed suit with the *Flaggenbuch*, the best flag book of all. Although the French and British naval authorities published several updated versions, even after World War II, they never approached the perfection of the *Flaggenbuch*, edited by Ottfried Neubecker and published in 1939.

Since the late 19th century manufacturers of cigarettes, tea and chocolate have made a real contribution to the popularization of national flags and ensigns throughout the world. In the United States, Great Britain, Germany, the Netherlands and other countries cards or pieces of silk with pictures of various flags have been added to cigarette or cigar packets, boxes of tea and wrappers for sweets. Collectors could send for an album with additional information and, although some of the pictures were inaccurate, they were still of great documentary value. Worth mentioning are the sets produced in the 1900s by Players in Great Britain and the German sets produced in about 1930 by

◆ **OPPOSITE PAGE**
◆ **TOP**
Two pages from the book by J.W. Norie and augmented by J.S. Hobbs, 1848.

◆ **BOTTOM LEFT**
Plate from the album J.H. Colton's *Delineation of the Flags of all Nations*, 1862.

◆ **BOTTOM RIGHT**
Plate VIII from *Flags of All Nations* presented by J. & G. Stewart, Old Vatted Scotch Whiskey Merchants, Edinburgh, 1897.

◆ **RIGHT**
Page from the album *Pavillons des Puissances Maritimes*, 1819.

175

STANDARD

OF AUSTRIA

176

Emperor of Austria.

177

Austrian War.

178
Austrian Merchant.

179
Austrian Signal for a Pilot.

180
Frankfort.

181
Ragusa.

182
Venice War.

183
Venice Peace.

184
Wirtemberg.

185
Bavaria.

186
Saxony.

187
Mecklenburg.

188
Rostock.

189
Wismar.

190

STANDARD

OF SARDINIA

Merchant the same as Kingdom without the Crown.

191
Kingdom of Sardinia.

192
Island of Sardinia.

193
Sardinian Signal for a Pilot.

194
Monaco.

195
Lucca.

196
Carrara.

197
Genoa.

198
Nice.

AMERICAN PRESIDENT.
3

AMERICAN REVENUE.
7

AMERICAN JACK.
4

AMERICAN ADMIRAL.
5

AMERICAN COMMODORES PENNANT
6

UNITED STATES OF AMERICA
STANDARD & PENDANT.
1

COLTON'S
FLAGS
OF ALL NATIONS

PUBLISHED BY J.H.COLTON, 172, WILLIAM STREET,
NEW YORK. 2

U.S. QUARANTINE.
8

U.S. SIGNAL FOR PILOT.
9

MEXICAN.
10

CENTRAL AMERICA.
11

GUATEMALA.
12

PRINTED BY LANG & COOPER, 117 FULTON ST N.Y.   Entered according to Act of Congress in the Year 1862 by J.H.Colton, in the Clerks Office of the District Court of the Central States for the Southern District of New York.

Turkey
Ensign & Merchant 49

Roumania
Royal Standard 50

Roumania
Merchant 51

Servia
Royal Standard 52

Servia
Merchant 53

Montenegro
Princes Standard 54

Bulgaria
Merchant 55

Greece
Royal Standard 56

Greece
Merchant 57

Persia
Royal Standard 58

Persia
Merchant 59

Siam
Royal Standard 60

Danzig

◆ **ABOVE**
Plate 58 from the album,
Flags of Maritime Nations,
Washington, 1899.

◆ **ABOVE RIGHT**
This plate with the flags of
the Free City of Danzig had
been prepared for the
Flaggenbuch, 1939, and was
removed at the last moment
(together with three plates
of the flags of Poland).

Bulgaria Cigarettes (*Flaggen der Welt*) and
Massary Cigarettes (*Wer nent die Länder, kennt
die Fahnen?*). Particularly valuable are the card
sets edited by O. Neubecker, the foremost
German flag authority, *Länder, Wappen und
Nationalfarben* and *Flaggen der Welt*. The set
produced by Sultan cigarettes from Dresden to
celebrate Germany's hosting of the 1936
Olympic Games in Berlin contains flawless

information, and is also a real gem in the art of
printing; it was produced in consultation with
Karl Fachinger, the forerunner of vexillology.
The pictures and information contained in
two albums of cigarette cards, edited by
O. Neubecker and published in 1950 under
the title *Die Welt im bunten Flaggenbild*, are so
accurate that these books deserve to be among
the leading sources of vexillological knowledge.

◆ **RIGHT**
Abadie Papier-Geselschaft
A.G. in Vienna has provided
collectors with thousands of
cards featuring flags and
coats of arms. Among them
were pictures of some 130
military colours and
standards preserved in the
Heeresmuseum (in Vienna)
including this colour of the
Cisalpine Republic cavalry.

◆ **FAR RIGHT**
National flag of Yemen
(1927–1962) on a card
published in 1936 by Sultan
Zigarettenfabrik Aurelia
in Dresden.

In the 20th century several dozen general books on flags have been published, a few of which have made major contributions to vexillology. These are *Die Flagge* by Vice-Admiral R. Siegel, 1912; a special edition of the National Geographic Magazine, *Flags of the World*, 1917; *Fahnen und Flaggen* by O. Neubecker, 1939; *The Flag Book* by Preben Kannik (in Danish 1956; in English 1957), with several subsequent editions prepared by Christian Fogd Pedersen, the foremost Scandinavian vexillologue; and the comprehensive *Flags Through the Ages and Across the World* by Whitney Smith, 1975.

In 1962 Whitney Smith established the Flag Research Center in Massachusetts, USA, which was the first professional vexillological institute in the world. He coined the word "vexillology", which is now a generally accepted term and used in many languages. Since October 1961 he has published *The Flag Bulletin*, the most authoritative journal on vexillology. Together with O. Neubecker, Louis Mühlemann and Klaes Sierksma, Smith organized the first international vexillological congress in 1965 and established the International Federation of Vexillological Associations (FIAV). The current membership of FIAV comprises 39 vexillological associations and institutions from 24 countries in all six continents. Most publish newsletters, of which the most important are

the Swiss *Vexilla Helvetica*, the Italian *Vexilla Italica*, the Belgian *Vexilla Belgica*, the Czech *Vexilologie*, the Spanish *Banderas*, the South African *SAVA Newsletter*, the American *Raven*, the German *Der Flaggenkurier* and the Ukrainian *Znak*. *The Flag Bulletin* and the publications of these vexillological associations have contributed to the tremendous recent increase in vexillological knowledge.

BRITISCHES REICH
FLAGGE DES GENERAL-GOUVERNEURS VON INDIEN
Serie 76 (1—130) Bild 33

BRITISCHES REICH
FLAGGE DES GENERAL-GOUVERNEURS VON KANADA
Serie 76 (1—130) Bild 40

DEUTSCHES REICH
FREIE UND HANSESTADT LÜBECK
STAATSFLAGGE FÜR STAATS-FAHRZEUGE D. BINNENSCHIFFAHRT
(ältere Flagge)
Serie 2 (1—40) Bild 29

DEUTSCHES REICH
LÜBECK
DIENSTFLAGGE
FÜR STAATSFAHRZEUGE
DER SEESCHIFFAHRT
Serie 2 (1—40) Bild 30

Kambodja
(französisches
Protektorat)
Nationalflagge

Brasilien
Präsidentenflagge

China
Flagge
des Präsidenten

All About Flags

A flag may be defined as a piece of pliable material, attached at one end so as to move freely in the wind, serving as a sign or a decoration. This word is now common to the nations of north-western Europe (Danish and Norse Flag, *Swedish* Flagg, *German* Flagge, *Dutch* Vlag*), but it does not appear to have come into use in this particular meaning until the 16th century, and the etymology of it is obscure. Perhaps the most satisfactory of the derivations hitherto put forward is that of Professor Skeat, who derives it from the Middle English* flakken *to fly, one of a number of similar onomatopoeic words suggestive of the sound of something flapping in the wind. Its first appearance with a meaning coming within the above definition is a specific term denoting a rectangular piece of material attached by one vertical edge, flown at the masthead of a ship, as a symbol of nationality or leadership. Before the 17th century there was no generic term in the English language that covered the various forms – banners, ensigns, streamers, pendants, etc. – that are now generally included under the term "flag".*

W.G. PERRIN, *BRITISH FLAGS*, CAMBRIDGE 1922

Precise terminology is needed to describe the various characteristics of a flag: its shape, proportions, design and colours. There are many different types of flag, made of different materials and with various accessories. Even hoisting a flag can be done in various ways. In what follows it is assumed that the flag is hoisted on a vertical staff and is flying to the right of the staff. This is termed the obverse, the main side of the flag. In most cases the reverse is a mirror image of the obverse but some flags – mainly military

colours – have different obverse and reverse and are really two flags sewn back to back.

The usage of flags has changed radically over the centuries, but some flag customs and etiquette, for example flying a flag at half-mast, have become part of everyday consciousness. Understanding the symbolic language of national flags is particularly important in diplomatic contexts, and on many occasions in recent history serious conflicts have arisen through ignorance or misunderstanding.

◆ **LEFT**
A huge Tunisian flag is displayed in Marseilles, France, during the 1998 World Cup.

FLAG DESIGN

The first characteristic of a flag is its shape. Most ensigns and national flags are rectangular. Some ensigns are swallow-tailed or double swallow-tailed, two national flags are square and one consists of two triangles. Most yacht flags are triangular or swallow-tailed, and the flags used by the army and navy are much more diversified.

The second characteristic of a flag is its proportions, i.e. the ratio of the width to the length. The width is measured along the hoist,

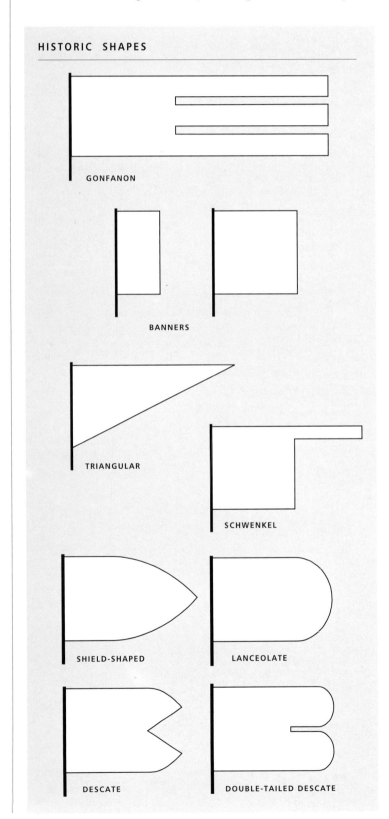

HISTORIC SHAPES

GONFANON

BANNERS

TRIANGULAR

SCHWENKEL

SHIELD-SHAPED

LANCEOLATE

DESCATE

DOUBLE-TAILED DESCATE

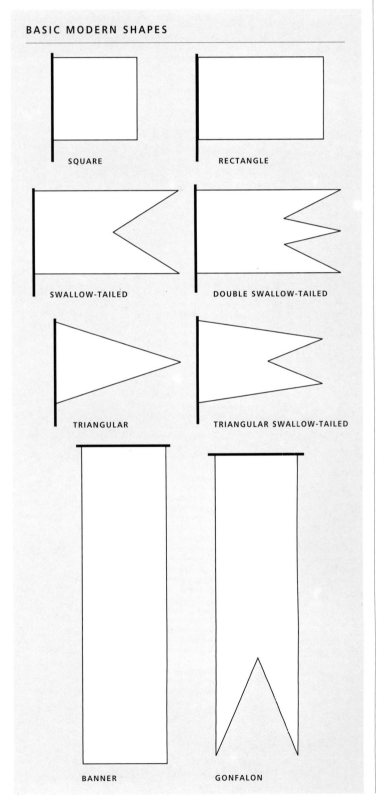

BASIC MODERN SHAPES

SQUARE

RECTANGLE

SWALLOW-TAILED

DOUBLE SWALLOW-TAILED

TRIANGULAR

TRIANGULAR SWALLOW-TAILED

BANNER

GONFALON

PARTS OF A FLAG

A — THE CENTRE
B — THE HOIST CENTRE
C — THE TOP CENTRE
D — THE FLY CENTRE
E — THE BOTTOM CENTRE

so it is the vertical measurement of a flag that is displayed horizontally and a horizontal measurement of a flag that is designed to hang vertically. The length is measured from the hoist to the fly end of a flag, and in triangular and swallow-tailed flags it is measured from the hoist to the apex of a triangle. For the sake of uniformity, organizers of international conferences and sports events usually adopt the same proportions for flags that are displayed together, although this can lead to distortion of the elements of the design. The correct way to present national flags on such occasions, and in flag charts and book illustrations, is to make all the hoists the same width and to retain the official proportions. In this arrangement, only the length of the flags will vary.

The third characteristic of a flag is its design. The terms for the basic parts of a flag are the "hoist" (first half), the "fly" (second half), "top"

(upper half) and "bottom" (lower half). In addition, there are terms for all the edges and particular points on the "field" (the whole area of the flag). In Europe many flags are historic armorial banners and therefore need to be described in heraldic terms; other flags display the coat of arms on a single-colour field. However, most flags have modern designs based on simple divisions of the field and/or display "simple charges" (simple figures).

Division of the field by horizontal or vertical lines results in horizontal or vertical stripes; dividing the field diagonally creates "bends". If these are of equal width, only their number is given in the flag's description. But if a design consists of stripes or bends of unequal size, the proportionate width must be quoted. For example, the description of the flag of Thailand is five horizontal stripes, 1:1:2:1:1, which means that the middle stripe is twice as wide as each of the outer stripes.

To divide the field into four parts a cross, or "saltire", is used. When the field is divided quarterly, the parts are called "quarters" and their colours are given in the following order: upper hoist, upper fly, lower hoist and lower fly. The colours of the triangles resulting from a division by saltire are given clockwise, beginning with the triangle based on the hoist.

The pieces of a chequered field are called "checks". The description of the field is given as follows: "checky a x b", where "a" is the number of checks in a horizontal line and "b" is their number in a vertical line. The field can also be divided with "gyrons"; there are normally eight or twelve. Their colours are given in a clockwise direction, beginning with the one

BASIC DIVISIONS

HORIZONTALLY

VERTICALLY

QUARTERLY

HORIZONTALLY TWICE

VERTICALLY TWICE

CHECKY

DIAGONALLY

DIAGONALLY TO LEFT

PER SALTIRE

DIAGONALLY TWICE

DIAGONALLY TWICE TO LEFT

GYRONNY

LINES:

WAVY

SERRATED

BASIC CHARGES

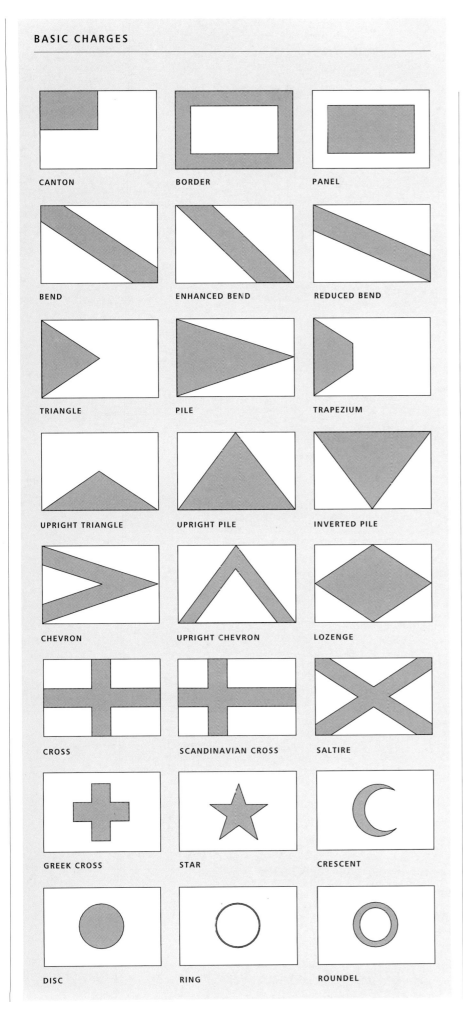

CANTON

BORDER

PANEL

BEND

ENHANCED BEND

REDUCED BEND

TRIANGLE

PILE

TRAPEZIUM

UPRIGHT TRIANGLE

UPRIGHT PILE

INVERTED PILE

CHEVRON

UPRIGHT CHEVRON

LOZENGE

CROSS

SCANDINAVIAN CROSS

SALTIRE

GREEK CROSS

STAR

CRESCENT

DISC

RING

ROUNDEL

whose longer edge coincides with the horizontal line dividing the hoist in half.

In most flag designs the division lines are straight, but in the design of some national, provincial and civic flags wavy and serrated lines are used. In heraldry there are more than a dozen other decorative lines of partition, which can be seen on armorial banners.

Most modern flags display charges, the most popular being cantons (squares or oblongs), stars, bends (diagonal stripes), crosses, triangles and piles (wedges). Charges such as a cross or bend are sometimes "fimbriated", i.e. edged with narrow stripes. Other charges such as a canton, pile or lozenge often carry another charge such as stars, a badge or other device. In medieval times the most widespread charges were crosses, lions, eagles and fleurs-de-lis, and today the most popular charge is a star. Before the American Revolution the stars that occasionally appeared on flags were heraldic stars with six or eight points. Since 1777, five-pointed stars have been used almost exclusively, and they currently appear on more than 50 national flags.

When a charge appears in a horizontal mirror position it is described as being "reversed". A charge pointing to the top of the flag is "upright" and one pointing to the bottom is "inverted". The width or diameter of charges is always quoted as a proportion of the width of the flag. The exceptions are a normal canton, a normal triangle and a pile. A normal canton covers the entire area of the upper hoist; if its dimensions are different, its proportion of the width of the flag is given. The apex of a normal triangle reaches the centre of the field; if the triangle reaches another point, it is specifically described by quoting the height of the triangle as a proportion of the width of the flag.

The next, very important, characteristic of a flag is its colour. Single colours or colour combinations are the main way a flag conveys its symbolic meaning. They may imply a political or religious ideology, symbolize national traditions or geographical features or, as in many European flags, display livery colours, i.e. heraldic tinctures that do not convey any symbolic meaning. There are seven heraldic tinctures, two "metals" and five "colours". The metals are gold (or) and silver (argent), represented on flags by yellow and white. The colours are red (gules), blue (azure), green (vert), black (sable) and purple (purpure). In Britain the livery colours are usually the first "metal" and the first "colour" mentioned in the "blazon" (a herald's description of a coat of arms), but in continental Europe the livery colours may be all the tinctures (three or four) of a coat of arms.

To simplify the description of livery colours, the International Federation of Vexillological Associations has adopted the following code:

R = red, O = orange, Y = yellow, V = green,
B = blue, P = purple, N = black, W = white,
Au = gold, Ag = silver, M = brown, G = grey.

There are also symbols for lighter and darker shades of colours:

– light, – – very light, + dark, ++ very dark

This code helps to give a rough idea about flag colours, but it is insufficient to describe specific shades such as United Nations blue, Kenya red, Qatar maroon or olive green.

Other basic rules of flag description are able to describe accurately only the simpler flags. To know the exact design and colouring of a particular flag, the reliable source of information is either the official government specification or a specification prepared by one of a few professional vexillologists. Such a specification should contain a large colour illustration of the flag together with enlarged details, accompanied by a description of the type of flag, dates of usage, proportions and exact colours given in the Pantone Matching System or CMYK (cyan, magenta, yellow, black), as used by printers and modern computer systems. Two examples are given here, the specification of the German fleet admiral made in the 1930s by the navy department in Berlin, and one of hundreds of flag specifications prepared by the Flag Design Center.

◆ BELOW LEFT
Flag of the German fleet admiral with construction details. Print of the German Admiralty, 1939.

◆ BELOW
Flag specification for the state flag of Germany (1935–1945) produced by the Flag Design Center.

GERMANY

State Flag

7 November 1935 (decree of 31 October 1935) – May 1945.

enlargements

A good flag design should be simple, yet distinctive and meaningful. As a medium of communication a flag must be easily recognizable. The divisions should be chosen not only for aesthetic value but also to enhance the flag's symbolic meaning. The emblems need to be large and as simple as possible, and should be placed in the most important parts of the field, such as the canton or centre of the flag. Light colours should be placed next to darker ones; no more than three colours should be used. Flags are employed as alternatives to written messages so should not bear any lettering or numbers. The reason, as in heraldry, is a practical one: colours and symbols are easier to "read" when a flag is seen from a distance or fluttering. It is also not a good idea to add a hatchment of arms or an armorial shield because the details would not be clear. The only effective way to make a coat of arms into a flag is as an armorial banner.

FLAG DESIGN GLOSSARY

Armorial banner A flag whose field consists of the field and charges of a coat of arms. In Great Britain the banner is square or rectangular (proportions 1:2), in Europe it is almost exclusively square

Badge A heraldic emblem, different from the coat of arms (it does not employ a shield)

Bicolour A flag with the field divided horizontally (horizontal bicolour), vertically (vertical bicolour) or diagonally (diagonal bicolour) into two equal parts in two different colours

Border A wide band surrounding a field of different colour

Breadth see *Width*

Canton The area of the upper hoist corner of a flag; also a square or rectangular field covering that area

Charge Any object placed on the field of a flag. The most common are charges that are based on a simple division of the field with straight lines. Frequently used charges are the star, cross, crescent, disc, fleur-de-lis and sun. Unlike the badge, the charge is not used separately

Checky A field bearing squares of alternating colours

Counterchanged Having two colours alternating on each side of a line drawn through a flag or arms

Crest An armorial figure attached to the helmet above the shield of a coat of arms. Sometimes used alone as a badge

Cross A charge in the form of a cross concentric with the field, its arms extending to the edges of the flag. See also *Greek*

Cross, Scandinavian Cross

Deface To add a badge or crest to a flag

Disc A circular device of a single colour used as a charge

Ensign-banner A rectangular flag with a field and fringe of livery colours of a coat of arms, charged with the full achievement of the arms

Field The whole area of a flag

Fimbriation A very narrow border of a simple geometric charge, usually in a contrast colour

Flammule A flame–shaped edge to a flag, often used in the past in the Far East

Fly The second half of the flag, the opposite end to the staff

Greek Cross A charge in the form of a cross with arms of equal length

Gyronny Divided into eight or twelve triangles whose apexes meet at the centre of the field

Hoist The half of a flag nearest the staff

Length The dimension of a flag measured from the heading or sleeve to the end of the fly; the opposite of *Width*

Livery colours The principal colours of a coat of arms. On a flag usually the first metal (gold or silver, i.e. yellow or white) is positioned above the first colour (red, blue, green, black or purple)

Obverse The more important, front side of a flag. It is the side to the observer's right from the staff; the opposite of *reverse*

Proportions The ratio of the width to the length of a flag. The proportions of a square flag are 1:1, a flag twice as long as it is wide is 1:2. The proportions of charges are always given in relation to the width of the flag

Quarterly Divided in four equal parts in a crosswise fashion

Reverse The less important side of a flag. It is the side to the observer's left from the staff; the opposite of *obverse*

Roundel A circular emblem of nationality employed on military aircraft and air force flags, usually consisting of concentric rings of national colours

Saltire A diagonal cross whose arms extend to the edges of a flag. Known also as a St Andrew's Cross

Scandinavian Cross A Latin cross positioned on the field of a flag horizontally, with the vertical arms in the hoist portion of the flag

Serrated A jagged division line or edge

Swallow-tailed A flag with a triangular section cut out from the fly end

Tricolour A flag whose field is divided horizontally (called a horizontal tricolour), vertically (vertical tricolour) or diagonally (diagonal tricolour) into three parts in three different colours

Triple swallow-tailed A flag with two symmetrical triangular sections cut out from the fly end

Union mark A symbol expressing the political unification of two territories, used in the canton of other flags. The most widespread is the British Union Jack

Width The measurement of a flag along its hoist; the opposite of *length*. In Commonwealth countries the British term "breadth" is used

TYPES OF FLAGS

"Flag" is an all-embracing general term used for a piece of fabric or other flexible material of distinctive design and coloration as a symbol of the identity of a nation, territory, office, corporation, organization, and so on. There are many types of flag, with different functions and usage as well as design and shape.

FLAG FUNCTION, USAGE AND SHAPE

The types of flags according to function are:
air force flag, armed forces flags, civil air flag, civil ensign, civil flag, colour, command pennant, commission pennant, courtesy flag, distinguishing flag, fanion, guidon, house flag, national ensign, national flag, naval reserve ensign, parley flag, pennon, pilot flag, rank flag, service ensign, signal flag, state ensign, state flag, war ensign;

The types of flags according to usage are:
banner, bannerol, car flag, courtesy flag, drum-banner, indoor flag, jack, lance pennon, outdoor flag, parade flag, parley flag, pipe-banner, table flag, trumpet-banner;

The types of flags according to shape are:
broad pennant, burgee, gonfalon, gonfanon, pennant, schwenkel, standard.

FLAG TYPES GLOSSARY

xAir force flag A special flag for use at a military airport

Armed forces flags Special flags for each part of the armed forces (army, navy, air force, marines). They are used to mark military garrisons and quarters, and during parades and ceremonies of a particular armed force

Banner (i) General term referring to a square or rectangular flag fastened to a staff or attached to a crossbar, having an armorial or other elaborate design and made of costly material, often hand-painted and/or embroidered. Unless the word is used figuratively, it is necessary to use a more specific term such as armorial banner, royal banner, civic banner, church banner, corporate banner, ensign banner, drum-banner, pipe-banner, trumpet-banner etc;
(ii) Any flag designed to hang vertically from a crossbar, with the design arranged accordingly. It is also called a hanging flag

BANNER OF RHINELAND-PALATINE IN GERMANY

Bannerol A small square flag charged with a single quartering of a deceased person and carried at his or her funeral; now obsolete

Battle honour A mark added to a colour or to a flag of a branch of the armed forces to show its military service

Broad pennant A tapering descate or swallow-tailed flag, mostly used by navies as the flag of the head of state. In British and American naval and yachting usage, it is the rank flag of a commodore

Burgee A small distinguishing flag of a club or individual yachtsman, usually either triangular or tapering swallow-tailed. Flown from the main mast, or from the bows in the case of a powerboat

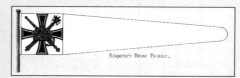

BROAD PENNANT OF THE EMPEROR OF GERMANY

Car flag Any flag flown from a car. Usually the flag of a head of state or government official, i.e. a rank flag or distinguishing flag. In most cases, it is displayed from a staff mounted on the right front fender. In the past it was on a staff clamped to a radiator cap

Civil air flag A flag for use at civil airports and landing fields

Civil ensign A flag designating national identity, flown on commercial or pleasure vessels. Formerly called a merchant flag

Civil flag A flag designating national identity, flown by private citizens on land

Club pennant A triangular flag to be hung vertically, usually charged with the emblem and livery colours of a sporting club

Cockade A rosette originally worn in a hat as a military badge, usually in livery or national colours. Since the 18th century also worn by civilians as an expression of revolutionary or patriotic feelings. In many European countries the first regulations pertaining to national colours related to the cockade, and later the colours of the cockade translated directly into a bicolour or tricolour flag

Colour Flag of a military unit (regiment, battalion or company). It usually has different designs on the obverse and reverse, and is fringed and attached to the staff

◆ LEFT
Parts of a military colour:
a finial
b bow
c cravat
d nails
e field
f fringe
g staff

Command pennant A flag identifying the commander of a particular navy formation (flotilla, squadron, group etc) or an individual ship. Usually triangular or tapering swallow-tailed

Commission pennant A very long, narrow flag (of proportions 1:15–1:50 or more), flown on a warship to indicate its commissioned status. If the ship's commander is of the rank of commodore or higher, the commission pennant is replaced by a rank flag. The term *Masthead pennant* is synonymous

COMMISSION PENNANT OF SAUDI ARABIA

Courtesy flag The civil ensign of a country being visited by a merchant vessel or yacht of a different nationality. Usually flown from the foremast or yardarm. It is hoisted on entering a foreign port

Desk flag See *Table flag*

DESK OR TABLE
FLAG, SLOVAKIA

Distinguishing flag A flag identifying a branch of government, military or naval service, or an official. In the latter case it denotes his or her office, authority, rank or command, and indicates his or her presence in a vessel, vehicle or place

Drum-banner A small flag decorating a parade drum. Used by a military, civic or other brass band parading in uniform or historic costume

Eagle (i) A vexilloid with a representation of an eagle on the top of the staff;
(ii) The name of the French colour during the Napoleonic era;

Ensign (i) A flag used to indicate the nationality of civil, government and naval vessels. Flown by ships at or near the stern. The term should always be preceded by an explanatory name (war ensign, civil ensign etc);
(ii) In the United States, the lowest commissioned officer in the navy;
(iii) In the 17th and 18th centuries, the usual term for a military colour and the colour-bearer

False colours An ensign worn by a ship not entitled to it

Fan A semi-circular patriotic decoration made of national flags or fabric in livery colours

Fanion (i) A small bicolour used for marking a position in surveying;
(ii) A small pennon in the regimental colours that is used on military vehicles for marker purposes

Flag This term most frequently refers to the rectangular flag used mainly on land by nations, government institutions, agencies and officials, provinces, cities, commercial firms, corporations, organizations, and so on

Flag of convenience The civil ensign of a country with low taxation and without stringent maritime regulations. The term applies to a ship whose owner is not a citizen of that country, but who registers the vessel there to avoid high taxes and in order to hire cheap labour

Gonfalon A long flag with a square or triangular tail, displayed from a crossbar. It originated in medieval Italy (a gonfaloniero was the person who carried such a flag), and is still used there by cities and communes. In other European countries it is used mainly by parishes and various religious associations

PERSIEN

Kaiserstandarte.

Standarte des Kronprinzen.

Standarte der Prinzen von Geblüt.

National- und Handelsflagge.

Dienstflagge.

Kriegsflagge.

Kommandowimpel,
mindestens fünfmal so lang als breit;
je länger die Fahrt, desto länger der Wimpel.

Gösch.

Kriegs- und Marineminister.

Übrige Minister.

Admiral.

Konteradmiral.

Befehlshaber der Marinestreitkräfte.

◆ LEFT
Distinguishing flags of Persia 1933–1958:
(*top row*) imperial standard, crown prince's standard, prince's standard;
(*2nd and 3rd flag in the 4th row*) ministers of defence or navy, other ministers;
(*5th row*) admiral, rear admiral, Commander of the navy.

Gonfanon Large lance flag with a square or rectangular field, and two to five squared long tails. The term derives from the Norse *gunn-fane*, which means a "war flag". In pre-heraldic and medieval times it was the flag of a ruler for carrying on horseback

Government flag see *State flag*

Guidon A small military flag, usually swallow-tailed or with a fly descate or cloven-descate, serving as a guide to troops. In Great Britain it was originally charged with the Union Flag in the hoist, and the badge and livery colours in the fly. Later guidons were charged with the arms

Hanging flag see *Banner*

Homeward-bound pennant United

- finial
- cord
- tassel
- fringe
- pole
- base

INDOOR FLAG

States term for the *paying-off pennant*

House flag The flag of a commercial firm flown at sea, and from its headquarters or branches on land

Indoor flag A flag made expressly for use in offices. It is made of more expensive fabric and the charge is often embroidered. It also differs from an outdoor flag by having a fringe, and it has a sleeve instead of the heading

Jack A small flag flown from a special jack-staff set in the bow of a warship. Usually hoisted when a warship is in harbour or lying in the roadstead. It may be a diminutive of the national flag, or of historic or other special design

LANCE PENNON
(JORDANIAN)

Jolly Roger Popular term for a black flag with a design in white referring to death. Modern flags show a skull and crossbones. The term was coined in the early 18th century for a flag used by pirates

Lance pennon A small flag, usually triangular or swallow-tailed, attached to the end of a lance

Masthead pennant see *Commission pennant*

Merchant flag see *Civil ensign*

Mourning ribbon Long black ribbon tied in a bow and attached to the staff just above the flag as a sign of mourning. An alternative to half–masting the flag

National flag (i) A flag of a nation-state, or formerly independent state, or of a non-independent national group that has its own government;
(ii) In the case of an independent state, a flag and ensign used by the government authorities, general public and the navy

Naval ensign see *War ensign*

Naval reserve ensign A flag used as a civil ensign on merchant vessels commanded by retired naval officers

OCCASIONAL FLAG – FLAG OF THE BICENTENNIAL OF THE AMERICAN REVOLUTION (1976)

Occasional flag A flag made for a particular occasion, such as an anniversary, holiday or international congress

Outdoor flag A flag made of stronger fabric with enforced edges and corners,

suitable for hoisting on flagstaffs and able to endure strong winds and inclement weather for a long period

Parade flag A flag to be carried outdoors by a marcher, usually made in the same way as an indoor flag

Parley flag A plain white flag displayed by combatants to request a ceasefire and to indicate the desire to negotiate terms of surrender

Paying-off pennant A commission pennant of a vessel returning home after a long period of service. It has up to 75 m (82 yd) of extra material added to the length

Pendant see *Pennant*

Pennant This is a general term for flags that are tapering, triangular or swallow-tailed in shape, originally flown from a crossbar and in modern times also flown from a vertical staff. Pennants differ from flags mainly in shape, size and manner of display. They originated at sea and some are used in this way (*Broad pennant, Commission pennant, Burgee*). There are, however, many more types of pennants for use on land, mainly as award and souvenir flags of corporate bodies and of sports, fraternal and other organizations

Pennon In medieval times a small personal flag of the arms-bearer below the rank of knight-banneret, intended for use on a lance borne by a mounted warrior. A pennon bore the arms in such a way that they were upright when the lance was in a horizontal position. In Britain since Tudor times pennons have consisted of the livery colours charged with a badge

Pilot flag A flag flown by a vessel requiring or carrying a pilot. Some countries have a special flag for this purpose, but in many others the "G" of the International Code of Signals is used

- grommet
- appliquéd eagle
- heading
- hem
- sewn chevrons
- hem

◆ **RIGHT** OUTDOOR FLAG: FLAG OF THE FLAG DESIGN CENTER

Pinsil Scottish triangular flag of proportions 4:9 with a fringe of the livery colours, charged with the crest and a strap badge in the hoist, and a plant badge in the fly. Used as a rallying point by a clan captain in the absence of the clan chief

Pipe-banner A small banner attached to the drone pipes of bagpipes. Military pipe-banners are two-sided, the obverse being charged with the regimental badge and the reverse with the company commander's arms

Quarantine flag A yellow flag flown by a ship that has not yet received medical clearance on arrival. It is the request for a certificate of good health

Rank flag A distinguishing flag indicating the rank of the officer of the navy (commodore to fleet admiral), army or air force (generals)

Regimental colour see *Colour*

Schwenkel A rectangular or triangular tail extending from the upper fly corner of a flag, or a strip along the top edge of a flag, with a dependent tail. Common in medieval

FLAG OF ZÜRICH WITH SCHWENKEL, 15TH CENTURY

Europe, now obsolete. The term is also means a whole flag with a schwenkel

Service ensign An ensign designated to identify a vessel, providing a particular service for customs, mail, fishery inspection, lighthouse service, environmental protection, and so on

Signal flag A flag used to transmit messages, especially at sea. The most widely used are the flags of the International Code of Signals

TRADITIONAL DESIGN OF AN ENGLISH HERALDIC STANDARD

Standard (i) A vexilloid used by the army; (ii) A long, tapering descate flag of heraldic design. Size varied according to the person's rank i.e. the length ranged from 7.3 m (8 yd) for the King to 3.5 m (4 yd) for a knight; (iii) A rectangular flag of heraldic design which is not an armorial banner; (iv) A flag of a head of state

State ensign A flag designating national identity, flown on non-military vessels in government service. Also called a *Government ensign*

State flag A flag designating national identity, used by government authorities and institutions on land. Also called a *Government flag*

Streamer (i) A long ribbon attached to the staff, which is used mainly in the form of battle honours; (ii) A long, narrow pennant used until the 17th century as a decoration on vessels

Table flag A small flag hanging vertically from a crossbar or attached to the staff with a stand. Used during international conferences and document signing ceremonies, or on a desk

Trumpet banner A small flag to decorate a ceremonial trumpet, usually a proper armorial banner. Used by a military, civic or other brass band parading in uniform or historic costume

Vane (i) A small metal flag set to swivel on a rod, mainly to indicate wind-direction. Usually attached to a steeple or roof; (ii) A short pennant used in the 17th and 18th centuries by merchant and naval vessels at each mast where no proper pennant was flying

Vexilloid This serves the same purpose as a flag but differs from it in appearance. It consists of a wooden or metal staff topped by an emblem made of animal bones, feathers, hide, wood or metal

Vexillum A square piece of cloth fastened to a crossbar, the standard of the Roman cavalry

War ensign The naval flag of a nation, also called a naval ensign. Carried by warships at or near the stern

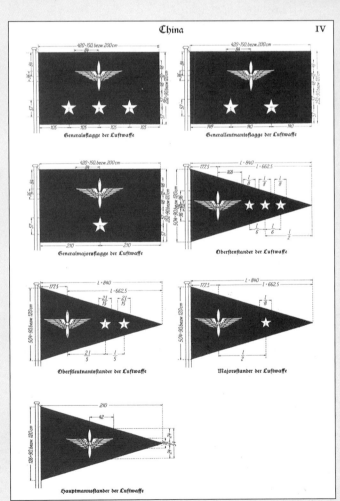

RANK FLAGS OF THE CHINESE AIR FORCE, PLATE FROM THE FLAGGENBUCH, BERLIN 1939

TRUMPET BANNER WITH THE ARMS OF FLORENCE CARRIED BY TRUMPETERS IN HISTORIC COSTUMES IN A PARADE PROCEEDING AN HISTORICAL SOCCER GAME

MATERIALS AND TECHNIQUES

The earliest flags were usually made of wool or silk. By the 13th century, the banners of rulers and the military were made of silk taffeta, and after the 15th century of silk damask. From the early Middle Ages these silk fabrics were decorated with colourful designs created using appliqué, gold leaf, chain stitch or flat stitch, or a combination of these techniques. From the 14th to the 16th centuries the ornamentation became more elaborate, featuring emblems of painted leather, delicate embroidery and pearls. From the end of the 16th century through to the 19th century most flags were painted and/or embroidered. The seams of ceremonial banners were often trimmed with silver or gold cord; the cantons or fields were adorned with relief embroidery and decorated with pearls and small gold spangles. The finest examples of craftsmanship are the so-called Julius banners, the war flags presented by Pope Julius II to the Swiss in 1512 as a token of appreciation for the Protectors of the Liberty of the Church.

◆ **ABOVE**
Relief embroidery has been used on the canton of the Julius banner of Basel (1512).

◆ **LEFT**
Large parts of the Madonna with Child, as well as the canton and letters on the border, are painted with gold leaf on the Julius banner of Schwyz (1512).

◆ **LEFT**
An example of a printed flag
is the civic flag of the city of
Lubin in Poland.

More general purpose flags, used by the army on land and by merchant or war vessels at sea, were made of cheaper fabrics, mostly rough or fine linen. Sendal was another popular fabric. From the 17th to the 19th centuries most ensigns were made of bunting and the emblems were painted or appliquéd on to it.

Only in recent years have fabrics been developed that can fulfil the numerous requirements of outdoor flags. The fabric has to give the flag a lustrous appearance at the same time as superb wearing strength, and it must also be washable, fire-resistant, mildew-resistant and mothproof. The flag should be light and able to fly well, even in rain, and both the fabric and the durable, fast colours must be able to resist high winds, intense sun, dirt and air pollution. Ideal fabrics for this have proved to be heavyweight, two-ply polyester or fabrics made of 25 per cent wool and 75 per cent nylon.

The designs on flags for outdoor use are normally sewn together; simple charges are appliquéd on, intricate ones are dyed and sewn. When many flags of the same design are required, they are dyed in large silkscreen workshops equipped with rows of tables 30–50 m (33–55 yd) in length. The chemical dyes, identical to those used in textile mills, are applied one colour at a time and penetrate the fibres so well that it is almost impossible to tell which side of the fabric is the reverse. Some flag emblems are larger than the silkscreen tables, so they have to be hand-painted using special paint. To assemble the flags, pieces of fabric in different colours are joined together with double

◆ **BELOW**
Hand-painted seal of Idaho
for a flag of 6 m (6½ yd) hoist.

seams using colour-matched thread. The top and bottom hems are made with two rows of stitching, while the fly-end hem has four rows of lock stitching with back-stitch reinforcement. Sometimes there are also several diagonal rows of stitching in the fly corners. The hoist is usually inserted and sewn into a heavy white canvas heading, either with grommets or with the rope sewn in. In Japan, instead of the heading, triangular pieces of canvas are used to reinforce the hoist corners.

The fabrics used for colours and for indoor and parade flags need to be particularly lustrous, with a surface suitable for embroidery. Embroidery is ideal for intricate multicoloured

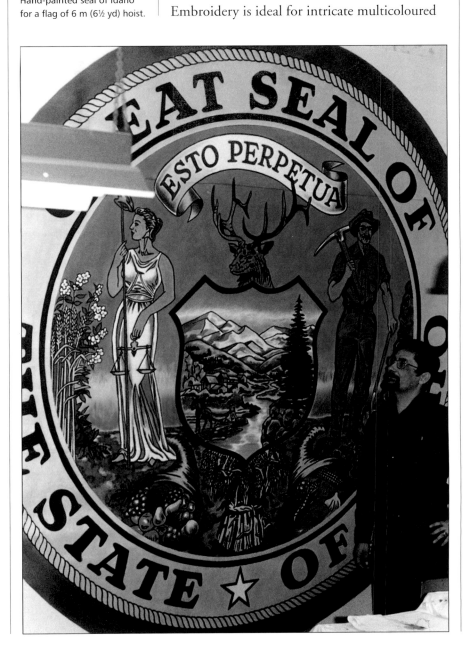

◆ **BELOW**
Detail of modern embroidery
with silver metal thread.

designs, and in recent years more and more flag manufacturers are using computer–aided embroidery machines. In the United States the stars of the national flag are embroidered on huge machines that are capable of producing hundreds of star fields simultaneously.

Large flag manufacturers have well-organized production lines, which begin at the art department where paper patterns of flag designs are prepared and stored. In a sewn flag, the relevant pattern is sent to the cutting department, which provides the sewing department with pieces of fabric in the exact sizes and colours needed. Once the pieces of fabric have been stitched together, the emblems are applied on top. Simple pre-cut emblems such as stars, fleurs-de-lis, crescents and crosses are pasted on and large emblems are then reinforced by stitching around the edges. In the finishing department the heading and grommets are added to outdoor flags, and indoor and parade flags are fitted with tabs and fringes.

MATERIALS GLOSSARY

Bunting A traditional all-wool fabric used for making flags from the 17th century to the present day

Calico A plain-woven cotton fabric of Indian origin. Used in the 17th and 18th centuries in Europe for some flags

Cotton A fabric made from the seed fibres of a variety of cotton plants native to most sub-tropical countries. Flag manufacturers use mercerized cotton because of its greater strength and lustre, and modern finishing processes make it resistant to stains, water and mildew. Widely used to make relatively inexpensive outdoor flags

Damask A patterned material, originally made of silk, which originated in the Middle East and was introduced to Europe by the Crusaders in the 11th century. Single damask has one set of warp and weft threads, and can be woven in one or two colours; double damask has a greater number of weft threads

Linen A cloth woven from flax, a plant of the family *Linaceae*. Flax is the oldest textile fibre, used in Anatolia for making clothes in the early Neolithic period, around 8000 BC

Nylon A synthetic plastic material manufactured since the late 1930s as a fibre from long-chain polyamides. Resistant to wear, heat and chemicals. Nylon taffeta is used to manufacture indoor and parade flags and heavyweight nylon is used for outdoor flags

Polyester A material manufactured from Terylene (Dacron) fibres, for which the basis is a long-chain polyester made from organic chemicals (ethylene glycol and terephthalic acid). Very durable, elastic, non-combustible and resistant to chemicals and micro-organisms, but prolonged exposure to even minimal sunlight affects colours

Rayon An artificial silk material, woven from fibres produced from the plant substance cellulose since the end of the 19th century. Used mainly to manufacture smaller dyed flags, 10 x 15 cm to 60 x 90 cm (4 x 6 in to 24 x 36 in). Heavy Bemberg rayon is used for the most luxurious indoor and parade flags

Sendal A fabric with a linen warp and silk weft. Used in northern Europe since the 13th century. It is suitable for painted heraldic banners

Silk A lightweight fabric woven from the filament of cocoons produced by the caterpillars of a few moth species belonging to the genus *Bombyx*. Relatively strong with a smooth, lustrous surface. Silkweaving originated in China in 2600 BC, and was known in Egypt from at least 1000 BC, and since the 12th century in Italy

Taffeta A plain-weave fabric, made of silk or nylon fibres, in which the warp and weft threads are evenly interlaced. Fine with a lustrous surface. Used mainly for indoor and parade flags, and colours

FLAG PARTS AND ACCESSORIES

Most of the accessories on flags for outdoor use constitute part of the design; the two that do not are the canvas heading and the hoist rope or grommets.

Indoor flags have various devices to attach the flag to the staff. These differ from country to country. The most popular device is a sleeve, which in Europe is fastened to the staff with special decorative nails. These nails bear engraved emblems with the names of the institutions or individuals who founded the flag or colour. In the United States of America the sleeve has leather tabs at each end, which attach to screwheads protruding from the staff. In Japan, instead of a sleeve, there are two or three leather triangles with eyelets that enable the flag to be fastened to the staff with decorative tasselled cords. Indoor flags will often also feature a fringe, a decorative tasselled cord and a cravat or the ribbons of an order.

◆ **LEFT**
Japanese flag for indoor or ceremonial use.

◆ **BELOW LEFT**
Heading with a hoist rope, ring and clip. Jack of Saudi Arabia (since 1981).

◆ **BELOW RIGHT**
Heading with a hoist rope and becket. Polish jack (1919–1945 and 1959–1993).

FLAG ACCESSORIES GLOSSARY

Cord A decorative, flexible string or rope made from several twisted strands. When attached to a ferrule, it has tassels and is tied in the middle. Used also to finish the edges of a flag. Usually of gold or silver thread, or in national livery colours

Cravat A wide ribbon attached to a staff below the finial, used as a distinction or as a mark of honour with a military colour or flag. Usually in national livery colours and richly decorated

Ferrule A metal ring at the top end of the staff, just below the finial

Finial An ornament on the top of the staff. Usually made of metal in the form of a spearhead, armorial crest or other three-dimensional figure

Fringe A decoration made of twisted thread or metal (gold or silver). Usually attached to the edges of the flag on the three free sides. Appropriate for indoor flags, parade flags and car flags

Grommet A metal eyelet reinforcing a hole near both ends of the heading, through

FINIAL OF THE FRENCH COLOUR OF THE 2ND REPUBLIC (1848–1851)

which clips are attached to a halyard pass

Heading A piece of canvas into which the hoist edge of a flag is sewn. To facilitate hoisting, it may have a rope sewn in or grommets fastened near the upper and lower edge

Sleeve A tube of material along the hoist of a flag through which the staff is passed. Used mainly for a colour or an indoor or parade flag

Staff A cylindrical piece of wood to which the flag is fastened. The staff of a colour is usually made of two pieces connected with a metal tube. See also *Finial; Crossbar, Flagpole, Gaff (Hardware Glossary)*

Tab A small piece of leather sewn inside the sleeve near both ends. When fastened to a screwhead protruding from the staff, it prevents the flag from slipping on the staff

Tassel A tuft of loosely hanging twisted threads or metal hanging from a cord attached to the staff. Used with a colour, or other ceremonial or decorative flag. Without a cord, tassels are also used at the points of a triangular or tailed flag hung vertically

FLAG HARDWARE

It would not be possible to display a flag without a few pieces of specially designed hardware. Beckets and toggles, rings and snaps, grommets and Inglefield clips all allow a flag to be fastened to the rope. Flagpoles make it possible to fly a flag at the desired height whilst flag belts enable someone to carry a heavy parade flag or colour more easily.

There are several ways of fastening a flag to a flagpole. In Europe a rope is sewn into the heading and attached to the halyard with a becket and toggle. Some flags, especially those for use at sea, have looped clips and Inglefield clips instead of beckets and toggles. In the United States brass grommets are inserted on each end of the heading, and the halyard is furnished with clips that attach to the grommets. In Japan the hoist edges are reinforced with triangles of heavy canvas with ribbons, which attach the flag to clips on the halyard.

A flagpole consists of a pole made of glass fibre, aluminium, steel or wood, with a truck on the top. Above the truck is a cap in the form of a disc, ball, eagle or other figure. The bottom part of the flagpole is embedded in a ground socket in a concrete foundation, or permanently welded to a base made of heavy cast aluminium. The halyard passes through a pulley in the truck and is secured to a cleat on the lower part of the flagpole. To prevent malicious damage or theft of flags, modern flagpoles are fitted with an internal halyard system and an access door with a lock. Older flagpoles can be modified with the addition of halyard covers and cleat-cover lock boxes. In cities, outrigger staffs or vertical flagpoles are usually set into a wall. They are constructed in a similar way to flagpoles, but the lower part is mounted in a metal base fastened with anchor bolts through the wall. Much smaller and lighter outrigger staffs are used by private home-owners who are well served by buying an inexpensive kit containing a sectional aluminium staff about 2 m (6 ft) long and a steel mounting bracket with screws.

FLAG HARDWARE GLOSSARY

Becket A loop at the end of a hoist rope that fastens to a toggle at the end of the halyard, making it easier to bend on a flag

Case A narrow sack to protect a parade flag in inclement weather, or to store it when not in use

Cleat A metal device with two arms, attached to the lower part of a flagstaff, to which the halyards are made fast

Crossbar A rod bearing a flag (usually a pennant, banner or gonfalon), attached directly or by a rope to a staff. The crossbar usually passes through the sleeve. Parts of the sleeve can be cut out to reveal parts of the crossbar

CLEAT

Flagpole A pole made of wood, metal or glass fibre on which a flag may be hoisted. It may be upright or projecting at an angle from a wall. Sometimes an upright flagpole is fitted with a yardarm or gaff to increase the number of flags that may be hoisted.

This practice is found mainly at naval establishments ashore

Flagstaff see *Flagpole*

Frame A wood or metal device designed to hold the top edge of a flag

Gaff A spar from which a flag is hoisted. It is set diagonally on the aft side of a mast. A flag is attached to a halyard passing through the outer end of the gaff. An ensign is flown from the gaff of the mizzen mast, or of the main mast in a two-masted ship

Halyard The rope to which a flag is bent in order to be hoisted

Inglefield clips Interlocking metal clips used to attach a flag securely to the halyard. Their quick-release mechanism makes it possible to bend on a flag easily

Mast A long, upright post of timber or metal set up on a ship or on a building

Staff see *Flagpole*

Tangle rod A metal device attached to a staff projecting at an angle from a wall, which clasps a flag and prevents it from wrapping around the staff

Toggle A device at the end of a rope sewn into the heading, consisting of an oval-shaped wooden or plastic crosspiece that fastens to a becket at the end of the halyard, making it easier to bend on a flag

TOGGLE

Truck A circular metal cap fixed on the head of a flagpole below the finial. It contains a pulley over which the halyard passes

Yardarm A bar attached horizontally to a mast of a ship or to a flagpole on shore to increase the number of flags that may be hoisted, attached to separate halyards

Usage and custom: on land

From time immemorial flags and banners were used to distinguish bodies of troops and to serve as rallying points when they needed to regroup or retreat. In the Middle Ages the number of banners carried into battle was imposing. There were royal banners, banners of provinces, cities and guilds, and banners of knights who were able to raise their own troops. At Buironfosse, where in 1339 the French and English Armies did not dare to stage battle, the French forces displayed 220 banners and 560 pennons, while the English had 74 banners and 230 pennons. In the battle of Tannenberg in 1410, the 56 banners unfurled by the Teutonic knights and the 91 banners by the Polish–Lithuanian forces were mainly the emblems of cities and provinces. Banners like these continued to be used on the battlefield until the 16th century, when European countries began to build standing armies based on permanent groupings of troops in legions and regiments.

After this date banners began to lose their heraldic character and by the beginning of the 17th century most of them displayed instead painted representations of patron saints or allegorical figures. Gradually all countries began to follow the example set by the French in 1597 and developed consistent designs for their infantry colours and cavalry standards. Military colours served their purpose on the battlefield until the end of the 19th century, when modern warfare made the function of colours in battle obsolete. (Several instances of troops displaying their colours were still reported even in World War II.) Today military colours are displayed only during military or state ceremonies.

In the Middle Ages banners were not only used in battle, however. In peacetime they were proudly displayed on the towers of castles and city halls, carried in triumphal marches and processions, and exhibited during all manner of festivities. The whole life of a banner was closely connected with the local church; every battle banner was consecrated in the church, was kept there in peacetime and was deposited there when it could no longer serve its purpose. Most

of the banners used on the battlefield in the Middle Ages served later to identify states, provinces, cities and guilds, and to this day many cities in Central Europe and Italy use the same flags as in medieval times.

Until the 19th century, the use of flags on land was limited and only a few countries had a national flag. The radical changes in the world that led to the revolutions in Europe of 1848 gave birth to the idea of the nation-state and from then on, in many sovereign countries, the civil ensign became the national flag.

In the same way that the coat of arms had been the sign identified with the ruler and the state, so the national flag was from the beginning a symbol with which people could identify. The concept of a national flag as a symbol of the people rather than the state became prevalent, and in many cases the flag was introduced by leaders of independence movements, revolutionaries or students and was only later officially adopted by government. The case of the British Union Jack, which to this day has never officially been declared to be the national flag, is proof that for the people of a

◆ **ABOVE**
Armorial banners of Bavaria, Brunswick and Saxony carried in the triumphal procession of the Emperor of Germany Maximilian I at the beginning of the 16th century.

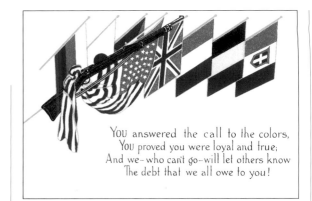

◆ **LEFT**
British recruitment poster,
World War I.

◆ **RIGHT**
American patriotic postcard,
World War I.

◆ **ABOVE**
British match label.

country legislative action is less important than their feelings. Almost everywhere in the world the national flag is not just a piece of bunting but something so close to people's hearts that they will risk their lives for it. Under foreign occupation, to display the national flag has often been an offence punishable by death, yet there have always been people defiantly hoisting their flag as a strong message that says, "This is our country, we are here to stay and we shall overcome!"

Awareness that the flag is a powerful symbol has induced totalitarian and oppressive regimes to de-legalize the flags of their opponents and to persecute those who defy the ban. In Spain, for example, it was illegal under Franco's regime to display the Basque flag. In answer to this, the Basque separatists hoisted a booby-

trapped flag that would blow up when the police tried to remove it. Israeli authorities have for decades harshly persecuted Palestinians caught with the flag of Palestine, and in the Soviet Union people could be sent to a concentration camp for publicly displaying the national flag of Lithuania, Armenia or any other nation that had been forcibly incorporated into the Soviet Union.

To sustain patriotic feelings during the Civil War in the United States, both sides published postcards of the national and Confederate flags, featuring allegorical figures of Liberty. In most of the countries involved in World War I, patriotic cards and posters displayed the national flag and the flags of the Allies. The message was clear: we fight for our country and have foreign friends on our side.

◆ **LEFT**
Flag mutilated during a street demonstration.

◆ **RIGHT**
Flag burning in Warsaw, 1998. Photo courtesy of Miroslaw Stelmach.

◆ **ABOVE LEFT**
Swiss cantonal flags decorate streets of all their cities, as shown here in St Gallen.

◆ **ABOVE RIGHT**
National flags at the UN headquarters in New York.

◆ **RIGHT**
Apollo 12 astronaut with United States flag on the moon, 28 November 1969. Photo courtesy of NASA.

◆ **BELOW LEFT**
The national flag of Switzerland at the head of an unusual parade.

◆ **BELOW RIGHT**
National flags displayed in the lobby of the State Department in Washington DC, 1986.

A common form of protest against the actions of a foreign country is to publicly burn its national flag. Left-wing students in France burnt the German flag as a protest against the arrest of Red Brigade terrorists. In many countries in the West, refugees from countries subjugated by the Soviet Union have burnt the Soviet flag, and under the regime of Ayatollah Khomeini the Iranians burnt United States flags. Workers belonging to the Polish "Solidarity" trade unions burnt the European Union flag out of fear that they would lose their jobs if Poland joined the EEC.

A traditional custom involving the national flag is to symbolically plant it in places that are discovered or conquered. The British have taken the Union Jack to all parts of the world. Roald Amundsen in 1911 planted the Norwegian flag at the South Pole, and in 1953 Edmund Hillary and Sherpa Tenzing Norgay placed the flags of New Zealand and Nepal on top of Mount Everest. The United States flag was carried to the North Pole in 1909 by Robert E. Peary, and in 1969 Neil Armstrong and Edwin E. Aldrin took it to the moon.

The political changes and development of international contacts in the 20th century have had a great impact on the development of all kinds of flags. In 1900 there were 49 sovereign countries and by 1998 their number had grown to more than 200. Many of these new countries adopted not only a national flag but also

numerous government services flags, as well as ensigns and other flags for use at sea. Tens of thousands of new flags have been adopted by political parties, trade unions, firms and corporations, youth movements, universities, schools, and yacht and sporting clubs. Occasional flags are designed for anniversaries such as the bicentennials of the American and French Revolutions, and for Olympic Games and international congresses. In some countries there are also flags for special occasions such as Christmas, Easter, Hallowe'en, birthdays or the birth of a baby.

In most countries the daily display of flags is limited to the flags of the head of state, national and state flags, flags of government agencies and officers, flags of certain companies and the flags of political parties, but in some countries flags are almost everywhere. Probably the most flag-filled nation is Switzerland. There, at least three flags (national, that of the canton and that of the commune or town) are displayed together and

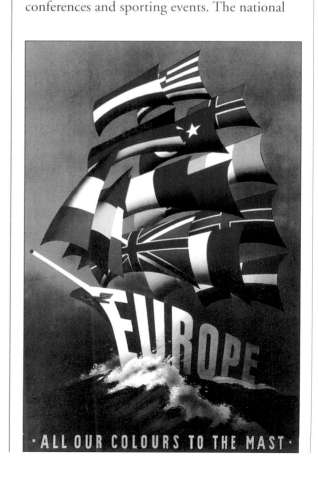

◆ ABOVE
Three flags from a match label set: Ethiopia (1941–1975); United States (1959); Laos (1952–1975).

◆ LEFT
This poster, produced in 1991 by Konstantin Geraymovich, was an expression of indignation of the Russian artist at the Soviet military intervention in the capital of Lithuania. The other two dates are those of Soviet invasions of Hungary (1956) and Czechoslovakia (1968).

◆ RIGHT
Flags used to great effect on a poster promoting the Marshall Plan, produced in 1950.

the larger streets in the cities are decorated with the national flag and the flags of all the cantons. National, provincial and civic flags, mostly in banner form, are permanently displayed in Germany. In the United States and Scandinavian countries the national flag is displayed not only by the authorities and public bodies, but also by a large part of the population in front of private houses. Throughout the world national flags are displayed on state holidays, and it is inconceivable to have street parades or demonstrations without a large number of flags. Hundreds of national or club flags are waved in stadiums and sports arenas by ardent fans, and in the 1990s the custom of painting the colours and design of the national flag on to the body developed.

The steadily increasing use of flags has been augmented by countless international meetings, conferences and sporting events. The national

· ALL OUR COLOURS TO THE MAST ·

◆ **RIGHT**
Crowds of supporters in Stockholm, Sweden, show allegiance to their national soccer team, 1994.

◆ **FAR RIGHT**
American soccer fans at the 1996 Olympics paint their faces with the stars and stripes.

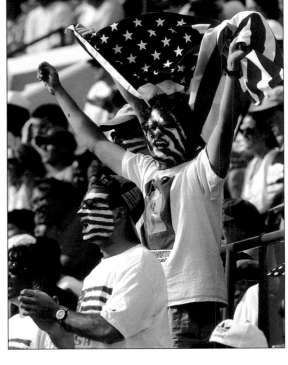

◆ **BELOW LEFT**
Commercial firms use flags in advertising to highlight the international scope of their business. This advertisement was for Stanwell of Denmark.

◆ **BELOW RIGHT**
Hotel sticker promoting the Albergo delle Nazioni in Florence, Italy.

flags of member-countries are permanently displayed at the headquarters of international organizations throughout the world, for example the United Nations in New York and the Commonwealth Institute in London.

The national flag as the visual symbol of a nation is so deeply engrained in modern consciousness that the media often show a flag as a symbol of a nation rather than just its name. Advertisers use pictures of national flags to suggest the international scope of their business, and large hotels eager to attract international clientele often display many different national flags. Most countries issue postage stamps to honour and promote their national flags. One of the first sets of stamps to illustrate flags in

colour was the famous American set of thirteen flags for the "Over-run Countries", issued in 1943–4. The largest series of 160 national flags was published by the United Nations in 1980–89. Sets of matchbox labels with national flags have been issued in Australia, Germany, Hungary, Spain and the former Yugoslavia. Flags also appear on lapel pins, ties and belt buckles, and on souvenir articles such as keyrings, T-shirts, mugs, umbrellas and playing cards.

USAGE AND CUSTOM: AT SEA

The first flags identifying nationality were used at sea. The oldest international legal obligation on record for ships to display flags as identification was agreed by King Edward I of England and Guy, Count of Flanders, in 1297. It explicitly compelled merchant ships to "carry in their ensigns or flags the arms of their own ports certifying their belonging to the said ports". From the beginning of the 13th century England claimed sovereignty over the seas and demanded that all ships belonging to other countries should salute the English ships by lowering their topsails, and later also by striking the flag. Captains who refused to do so were regarded as enemies and their ships and cargo forfeited. Foreign ships submitted because England insisted only on a salute and levied no duties on ships passing through the English Channel. The practice became obsolete in 1805, but the custom of saluting a foreign vessel remains to this day. Merchant ships salute each other by dipping the ensign as an act of courtesy; warships do not dip to each other, but if a merchant vessel dips to them they reply.

For a long time the national ensigns of the main maritime powers served as passports for merchant ships sailing to Turkey, North Africa, China and India. Under a treaty made by King Henry VI of France and Sultan Ahmed of the Turkish Empire, from 1604 to 1675 ships of all nations could visit the Turkish ports and trade there only "under the authorization and security of the Banner of France". The situation changed in 1675 when a British–Turkish capitulation treaty reserved the right to free trade in Turkey for the "English nation and the English Merchants and all other nations or Merchants who are or shall come under the banner and protection of England". Similar provisions concerning the protection of ships and citizens and/or free trade were included in treaties made between France and the Turkish vassal states in North Africa: Morocco (1682), Tripoli (1685) and Tunis (1685). Another example is Austria's peace treaties with Morocco and Turkey (1783–5). One of the purposes of these and subsequent treaties was to protect commercial shipping from pirates.

As well as the national ensign there were, and still are, many other flags for use on ships. The oldest is the jack, flown from the bow. Currently private ships display the civil ensign or service ensign on the stern, the house flag on the foremast and (in Britain) the jack on the bow. On sailing ships the civil ensign is often displayed from a halyard attached to the mizzen mast. Yachts fly the civil ensign on the stern and the club burgee or private flag on the mast. On war ships the war ensign is flown on the stern and the jack on the bow; on the main mast either the commission pennant or a command flag, with the rank flag below, is flown.

◆ **BELOW**
Flags on a warship.

commission pennant

rank flag

war ensign

jack

FLAG ETIQUETTE

There are no international regulations governing flag etiquette but the rules adopted by many countries have so much in common that it is possible to formulate general guidelines. They are slightly different for a flag displayed inside a country and for one at an international forum. The general rule in both cases is that all flags hoisted as a group should be the same width and should be hoisted on separate flagpoles, or separate halyards in the case of a flagpole with a yardarm. The practice of hoisting two or more flags on the same halyard is not correct.

In most countries the following rules are observed for hoisting flags inside the country:

✦ The flag should be displayed in the open from sunrise to sunset, but it should not be displayed on days when the weather is inclement. It may be displayed at night providing that it is well illuminated.

✦ The flag should be hoisted briskly and lowered ceremoniously.

✦ The flag should always be used in a dignified manner. It should never touch the ground, the floor or water. It should never be carried flat or horizontally, but always aloft and free. It should never be used as a table or seat cover, or as drapery of any sort. It should never be used as a receptacle for receiving, holding, carrying or delivering anything.

✦ The national flag should not be displayed in a position inferior to any other flag. The national flag takes precedence over all other flags. When flown with the flags of other sovereign nations, all flags should be flown on separate flagpoles of the same size. The flags should be of the same size or the same width, and should be flown at the same height. The other national flags should be displayed in alphabetical order according to the official language of the country.

✦ When there are two flags displayed, the national flag should be on the left of the observer, facing the staff. The same rule should be observed when the national flag is crossed with another flag; its staff should be

in front of the staff of another flag; see diagram overleaf.

✦ In a line of three flags, the national flag should be positioned in the centre; see diagram overleaf.

✦ In a line of four flags, the national flag should be the first to appear on the observer's left; see diagram overleaf.

✦ In a line of five or more flags, two national flags should be used, one at each end of the line; see diagram overleaf.

✦ In a semi-circle, the national flag should be in the centre; see diagram overleaf.

✦ In an enclosed circle, the national flag should be positioned and centred immediately opposite the main entrance to a building or arena; see diagram overleaf.

✦ The order of flags hoisted together depends on the place of each particular flag in the following hierarchy: (a) national flag, (b) regional or provincial flag, (c) county, parish or commune flag, (d) civic flag, (e) service flag (e.g. police, fire brigade), (f) other flags (university, school, commercial firm, sports club etc).

✦ When the national flag is carried in a procession it should always be aloft and free. In a single line the national flag must always lead. If carried in line abreast with one other flag, it should be on the right-hand end of the line facing the direction of movement; if carried with two or more other flags, it should either be in the centre, or two national flags should be displayed, one at each end of the line.

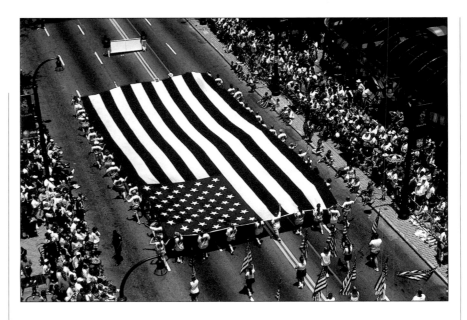

◆ **ABOVE**
A huge flag carried flat looks good from above, but since its design is not visible to the spectators standing on the ground it is not correct flag etiquette. In this example, the event is a 4th July parade in Georgia, USA.

45

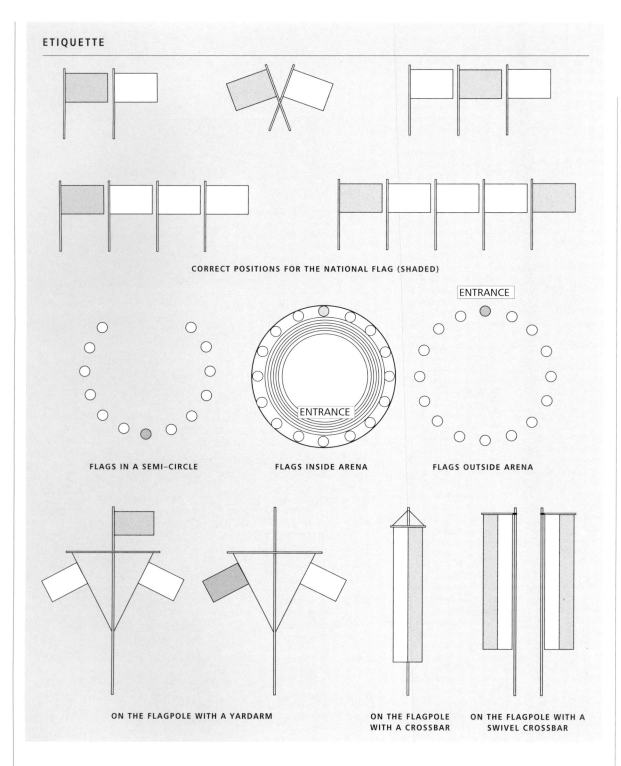

ETIQUETTE

CORRECT POSITIONS FOR THE NATIONAL FLAG (SHADED)

ENTRANCE

ENTRANCE

FLAGS IN A SEMI-CIRCLE

FLAGS INSIDE ARENA

FLAGS OUTSIDE ARENA

ON THE FLAGPOLE WITH A YARDARM

ON THE FLAGPOLE WITH A CROSSBAR

ON THE FLAGPOLE WITH A SWIVEL CROSSBAR

✦ The correct position of the national flag displayed on a flagpole fitted with a yardarm is illustrated above.

✦ When a flag is displayed over the middle of a street, it should be suspended vertically, with its top edge to the north in an east–west street or to the east in a north–south street.

✦ When a flag is displayed vertically on a flagpole with a crossbar, the upper edge of the flag is to be on the observer's left; see above.

✦ When a flag is displayed vertically on a flagpole with a swivel crossbar, the upper edge of the flag should face the flagpole; see illustration above.

✦ When a flag is displayed from a staff on a speaker's platform, it should be on the speaker's right as he faces the audience.

✦ When used to cover a coffin, a flag should be placed so that the hoist is at the head and the top edge is over the left shoulder.

✦ As a sign of mourning the flags on flagpoles are half-masted. A black ribbon is attached to flags hoisted on short outrigger staffs, and a black cravat to military parade flags.

Bend on a flag To fasten a flag to halyards in order to hoist it

Break out a flag To unfurl a flag that has been rolled and tied in such a way that a sharp tug on the halyard will cause it to open out

Consecration The dedication ceremony of a colour or other flag

Desecration Disrespectful treatment of a flag such as burning it in public, defacing it with inappropriate inscriptions or emblems, mutilating it, trampling it or throwing it on the floor or ground. Punishable in most countries of the world

Dip a flag The custom of lowering a flag briefly and temporarily in salute. A sign of respect used to honour the national anthem, an important person or another vessel

Drape a flag The custom of attaching a black cravat to a staff as a sign of mourning

Dress ship To decorate a vessel with flags for a holiday or special occasion. Until the 20th century all flags in the ship's store were raised on every available halyard but now only signal flags are displayed

Flag officer A naval officer entitled to use a rank flag, usually above the rank of captain

Fold a flag A ceremony performed after a flag is taken down from a flagpole or removed from a coffin it has covered. The flag is folded lengthwise three times in such a way that the upper hoist part is on the outside. A series of triangular folds follows, beginning at the fly, until the flag resembles a cocked hat with only part of the hoist still visible

Half-mast To fly a flag at a point much below its normal position, usually as a sign of mourning. The flag should be first hoisted to the peak for an instant then lowered to the half-mast position. It should be raised again to the peak before it is lowered for the day

Honour a flag Whenever a military unit or civil organization is awarded, the order ribbons are ceremoniously attached to the staff of the colour or banner. The head of state or his deputy personally presents the award at a ceremony held in the presence of the military unit or a representative of the organization

Lay up colours To deposit old colours ceremoniously in a church or museum

Pall flag A flag laid over a coffin, hearse or tomb. This is used mainly at government and military funerals. It is removed from the coffin before it is lowered into the grave

Salute the flag Flags are saluted when being hoisted, lowered or passed in a parade review. Civilians stand at attention, men remove their headgear and military personnel place the right hand to the head in a prescribed salute

◆ **LEFT**
Pall flag - Mother Theresa lying in state with the Indian national flag laid over her body, 1997.

✦ When a flag is no longer in a suitable condition to be used it should be destroyed in a dignified way by burning it privately. At the headquarters of international organizations and at international conferences or sports events, national flags should be arranged in alphabetical order, either in the official language of the host country or in English. National flags hoisted together should be the same width. When the flagpoles form an enclosed circle the order of flags should be clockwise, with the first flag positioned opposite the main entrance.

Flags are designed in such a way that they should be displayed in a horizontal position. There are, however, at least two circumstances when flags are displayed vertically: on a table (see *Types of Flags: Table flag*), and when they are positioned against a wall. In other circumstances vertical is an unsatisfactory way to display flags because coats of arms or emblems may lose their upright position. Indeed, at least four countries, namely Brazil, Pakistan, Saudi Arabia and Sri Lanka, explicitly forbid vertical display of their national flags. However, Liechtenstein, Slovakia and Slovenia have special designs for displaying their national flags in a vertical position, and Germany and Austria both have a custom of turning coats of arms upright in state flags that are hanging vertically. The general rule to be observed when a flag is displayed vertically is that the upper edge of the flag should be to the observer's left (the observer will see the reverse of the flag). The only exceptions are the flags of Liechtenstein, Slovakia and Slovenia, which should be displayed in accordance with their official designs for vertical flags.

FLAG CONFLICTS

The knowledge of flags and flag etiquette is a very important part of diplomatic protocol, unfortunately not always observed correctly. For example, the Iranian delegation to a European country almost abandoned talks because the hosts placed on their table the flag of Iran used by the overthrown Shah regime. An incorrect vertical display of some flags can cause serious consternation because the Polish flag becomes the flag of Monaco or Indonesia, the Dutch flag becomes that of Yugoslavia, the Russian flag changes into the Serbian flag and the civil flag of Ethiopia becomes that of Bolivia.

One of the first recorded incidents happened in September 1916 when King Vajiravudh (Rama VI) of Siam was visiting areas devastated by floods. All the towns and villages he visited were decorated with the national flag, red with a white elephant, but one was flying upside down. The sight of the elephant lying on its back shocked the King to such an extent that he decided to adopt a new flag with a simple design of red and white stripes that was incapable of being flown upside down.

Serious and long-lasting conflicts have been provoked by changing the national flag. The longest was the *Flaggenstreit* (flag conflict) in Germany after World War I. The struggle was between those who wanted to restore the

♦ **LEFT**
The national flag of Siam (Thailand) (until 1916).

♦ **LEFT**
The national flag and civil ensign of Siam (Thailand) (1916–1917).

tricolour of 1848 and those who wanted to keep the flag designed by Bismarck in 1867, so it was a conflict between the adherents of two ideologies. The black, red and yellow were perceived as the colours of the democratic republic, and of unity, law and freedom, whereas the black–white–red tricolour, combining the colours of Prussia (black and white) and Brandenburg (red and white), was a reminder of the glorious days of the empire dominated by the militant Prussia. The situation was so tense that the republican government decided on a compromise. The flag of 1848 was restored as

♦ **BELOW**
(left to right)
German national flag and civil ensign (1848–1866);
German national flag and civil ensign (1867–1919);
German civil ensign (1919–1933);
German civil ensign (1933–1945).

the national flag, but all flags for use at sea (civil ensign, state ensign, war ensign, jack) remained black–white–red, with the addition of the national colours in the canton. When Adolf Hitler came to power in 1933 the German flags were changed again. The black–white–red tricolour was reinstated as the national flag but it could be displayed only together with the

Hakenkreuzflagge of the Nazi Party. Two years later the *Hakenkreuzflagge* became the national flag and civil ensign, and the base for all other ensigns and flags of the Third Reich.

Similar, but less intense, conflicts occurred between supporters of the Union Jack and the proponents of a new national flag in South Africa in the 1920s, and in Canada in the 1960s. Currently there is conflict in Russia between the pro-democratic forces and the communists who want to restore the Soviet flag. In Belarus patriots are demonstrating under the

with the Olympic rings in white. Then, after Taiwan was denied its seat in the United Nations, the International Olympic Committee denied it the right to use its national flag at the Olympics and demanded that a special flag be designed for the Chinese–Taiwan Olympic team; it was carried for the first time at the 1984 Olympic Games. The flag is white with the national emblem and Olympic rings within a stylised five-petalled flower shape. For political reasons, the national flag of South Africa was also banned and the South African team was

◆ **ABOVE LEFT**
All-German Olympic flag (1959–1968).

◆ **ABOVE CENTRE**
The Taiwan Olympic flag (since 1984).

◆ **ABOVE RIGHT**
The flag of the South African team carried at the Summer Olympic games in Barcelona, Spain (1992).

historic flag against the president, who has decreed a flag similar to that used when Belarus was a Soviet republic.

In the 1990s flag conflicts were clearly visible during street demonstrations in Russia and Germany. In Russia the democrats march under the national flag, the communists under the Soviet flags and the Soviet war ensign, the monarchists under the black–gold–white tricolour or the national flag with the imperial eagle added, and the militant nationalists under the current war ensign. In Germany the militant neo-Nazis carry the imperial war ensign or flags of the *Freie Arbeitspartei*.

On the international scene, there have been several incidents at the Olympic Games. The first involved teams from both West and East Germany who were compelled to use the All-German Olympic flag (*Gesamtdeutsche Olympiaflagge*), the German flag defaced

compelled to use a special flag at the Olympic Games of 1992. At the same Olympics the teams from Bosnia and Herzegovina, Serbia and member-countries of the Commonwealth of Independent Countries were disqualified from holding any flags.

The latest flag conflict began in 1991 when Macedonia broke its ties with Yugoslavia and proclaimed an independent republic. As one of Greece's provinces is also named Macedonia, Greece began to contest the new country's right to this name. The Greek protests intensified in 1992 when Macedonia adopted a flag with the Star of Vergina, associated with King Philip II of Macedon and his son, Alexander III the Great (356–323 BC). Because a similar flag is used in Greek Macedonia, the Greek Prime Minister denounced the flag of Macedonia as a clear provocation. Because of the objections raised by Greece, Macedonia was admitted to the United Nations in April 1993 under the name "The Former Yugoslav Republic of Macedonia" and was denied the right to have its flag flown at the UN headquarters in New York, a move unprecedented in UN history.

◆ **BELOW**
The national flag of Macedonia (1992–1995).

Emperors, Sovereigns and Presidents

In the Middle Ages and much later in some countries, the state flag was the personal heraldic standard of the ruler. He was the state, and when his subjects went to battle or sailed the seas they flew his flag.

G.A. HAYES-MCCOY, *A HISTORY OF IRISH FLAGS*, BOSTON, 1979.

In the Middle Ages the ruler was regarded as the embodiment of the state, and for many centuries his banner was synonymous with the national flag. It marked his castle (or his tent in a military camp), was carried into battle and was flown on the masthead of his ships. Before the dawn of heraldry the personal flag of a ruler was plain red, showing that it was the flag of the emperor (*vexillo roseum imperiali*) or of someone with the right to govern in his name. Sometimes the red field of the emperor's flag was charged with a white cross as a sign that he had taken part in a crusade.

Diversification of these flags began in the second half of the 12th century when heraldic devices were introduced, and until the 15th century all of the flags of Europe's rulers were armorial banners. Most sovereigns continued to use armorial banners until the late 19th century, but in the 15th century the monarchs of southern Europe began to use unicolour royal flags, usually a white field carrying the royal coat of arms. At the end of the 17th century Scandinavian monarchs defaced their war ensigns with white panels bearing the whole arms, and a few further modifications have taken place during the last two centuries. These basic designs have served as the models for almost all the royal and presidential banners and flags in use throughout the world even to this day.

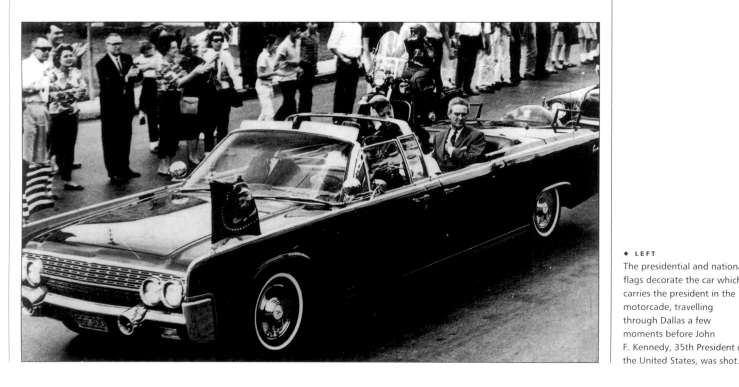

◆ **LEFT**
The presidential and national flags decorate the car which carries the president in the motorcade, travelling through Dallas a few moments before John F. Kennedy, 35th President of the United States, was shot.

MEDIEVAL EUROPE

In the course of the century from 1195 to 1295, most European rulers adopted coats of arms and armorial banners bearing one of the two most important heraldic figures: the lion, the king of the beasts, or the eagle, the king of heaven. There was the imperial black eagle, the three golden lions of England, the red lion of Scotland, the white lion of Bohemia, the black lion of Flanders, the purple lion of Leon, the three blue lions of Denmark, the lion with an axe of Norway and the white eagle of Poland.

In the Mediterranean region the King of Portugal in 1185 adopted a complex coat of arms displaying four blue shields forming a cross on a silver field, each shield charged with five white dots arranged in a saltire (diagonal cross).

◆ **LEFT**
Royal banners in 1300.

Holy Roman Empire.

England.

Scotland.

Denmark.

Norway.

Flanders.

Bohemia.

Poland.

Hungary.

France.

Portugal.

Spain.

51

The shields symbolize the five Moorish kings defeated by the Portuguese and the five dots refer to the five wounds of Christ. After the final annexation of Algarve and the wedding of the King to Beatriz of Castile, a red border charged with golden castles was added to the arms. The other three kingdoms on the Iberian Peninsula had quite simple arms. The arms of Castile were the canting arms, a golden castle on red; those of Aragon were four red pallets on red; and those of Navarre were a gold chain arranged per cross, per saltire and in orle (as a border), with an emerald at the centre, all on red. From 1230 to 1479 the Spanish coat of arms was quarterly Castile and León. The arms of Sicily were per saltire Aragon and Hohenstaufen (black eagle on white). The royal coat of arms of France was golden fleurs-de-lis on a blue field; until the end of the 14th century their number was not limited, thereafter it was reduced to three.

Although it was not a kingdom, one of the most important states of the medieval period was the domain of the Teutonic Order. The white banner of the Grand Master of the Order was charged with a yellow and black cross, with the arms of the Holy Roman Empire in the centre.

As we saw in the example of Spain, already by the 13th century a king ruling over more than one domain incorporated their arms in his coat of arms and on his banner. Where there were two territories, this was done by either quartering or impaling the shield. In the case of quartering, the first arms appeared in the first and fourth quarter, and the second arms in the second and third quarter. The arms impaled had the shield divided per pale (vertically), as in the arms of Hungary under the rule of the Anjou dynasty (1387–1437), which displayed the Hungarian arms and the arms of France. In time the number of shield divisions grew to accommodate the arms of the extra territories, but even so at the ruler's funeral the separate banners of all of his domains were carried as well as his state banner.

◆ **ABOVE**
(clockwise from top left)
Grand Master of the Teutonic Order; England (1405–1603); Hungary (1387–1437).

THE MODERN WORLD

An example of a quite complex armorial banner is that of Burgundy, which reunified in the 14th century and for more than 100 years was one of the richest countries of Europe. It extended its possessions northwards to Flanders, Brabant and Holland, but in the 1470s was torn apart by Austria and France. The banner of Burgundy is quarterly the arms of Burgundy Modern (first and fourth quarters), Burgundy Ancient impaling Brabant (second quarter) and Burgundy Ancient impaling Limburg (third quarter), and displays the arms of Flanders on an inescutcheon.

◆ ABOVE
Banner of Burgundy.

the arms of Aragon and Sicily; the arms of Granada were added in 1492, and the arms of Austria, Burgundy Modern, Burgundy Ancient, Brabant, Flanders and Tyrol in 1504. Since 1603 the British royal banner has displayed the arms of England together with those of Scotland and the Irish harp, and since 1714 also the arms of Hanover.

At the end of the 15th century the diversification of the personal flags of European rulers began. The armorial banner still usually

◆ ABOVE
Great Britain (1714–1801).

The expansion of the domains of other rulers was similarly reflected in their arms and banners. In 1438 Rudolf I of Habsburg was chosen to rule the Holy Roman Empire and Austria was established as his family's principal duchy. The imperial eagle was therefore ensigned in 1493 with the escutcheon of the arms of Austria, and from 1508 to 1519 the arms of Austria were impaled with those of Burgundy. Later the crowned eagle with a sword and a sceptre in its claws appeared on the imperial banner without the inescutcheon. In 1479 the kings of Spain augmented the arms of León and Castile with

◆ BELOW
Banner of the Duke of Brunswick-Lüneburg (1914–1918).

◆ **FAR LEFT**
Banner of the king of Saxony
(1815–1918).

◆ **LEFT**
Banner of the grand duke of
Mecklenburg (1900–1918).

◆ **BELOW LEFT**
Banner of the king of Bavaria
(1806–1835).

rulers for use at sea. The fields of these flags were white, the only exceptions being the yellow field of the imperial flags of Austria and Russia. Some later royal flags displayed the whole state arms on a red field.

In the 18th century Prussia emerged as one of the most powerful countries in Europe. Its arms had evolved from those of East Prussia, which was created by the secularization of the powerful

prevailed on land, but the Catholic monarchs of Spain introduced a white flag with the arms in the centre, designed for use at sea. In a few countries this kind of flag became the alternative personal flag of the ruler on land and thus the second model of the personal flag for heads of state came into being.

In the late 17th and 18th centuries the second model was adopted by most European

◆ **LEFT**
France, royal flag and ensign,
(17th to 18th century).

PAVILLON ROYAL DE FRANCE

PAVILLON ROIAL D'ESPAGNE

PAVILLON ROIAL DE PORTUGAL

◆ **FAR LEFT**
Spain, royal flag
(17th to 18th century).

◆ **LEFT**
Portugal, royal flag
(17th to 18th century).

◆ **RIGHT**
Austria (German emperor),
standard of the Emperor.

◆ **FAR RIGHT**
Tuscany, royal flag
(17th to 18th century).

◆ **FAR RIGHT**
Russia, standard of the
emperor (18th century).

◆ **BELOW**
Spanish royal standard
(1833–1868 and 1875–1931).

Teutonic Order. In 1525 the Grand Master of the Teutonic Order had sworn allegiance to King Sigismund the Old of Poland and had received from him a white banner defaced with the new arms of East Prussia: a black eagle with the royal crown on its neck, and the royal cipher "S" on its breast. In 1569 the cipher was replaced by the "SA" of the Polish King Sigismund August, and later it combined the letters of the Polish kings and the Prussian princes (VG for Vladislaus-Georgius and JCF for Johannes Casimirus-Frederick). In 1618 East Prussia came under the direct control of the electors of Brandenburg and the eagle was ensigned with their crown. When the kingdom of Prussia was proclaimed in 1713 the crown was replaced with the royal one and the cipher changed to "FR" (*Fredericus Rex*).

The other country to attain the position of a world power at this time was Russia, which at the beginning of the 18th century was modernized by Peter the Great. He introduced the yellow imperial banner with a representation of the state arms in the centre. The arms had been adopted by Ivan III after his marriage to Sophia Paleologue, a niece of the last Byzantine emperor, and were those of Byzantium – a golden double-headed eagle on a red field. In the 16th century this was defaced with the arms of Moscow (St George slaying the dragon) and at the end of the 17th century the colour of the eagle was changed to black and the field to gold.

In some countries until the end of the 18th century the ruler had at least two different flags and in many countries there was no special flag

◆ **ABOVE LEFT**
Royal flag of the Netherlands (1815–1840).

◆ **ABOVE CENTRE**
Royal flag of Afghanistan (1930–1973).

◆ **ABOVE RIGHT**
Imperial flag of Japan since the second half of the 19th century.

for the head of state. But in the 19th century the rulers and presidents of all countries began to adopt their flags.

The first presidential flag in the world followed the second model. It was a blue flag with the state arms of the United States in the centre, used on naval ships since the first half of the 19th century and made official in 1882. As commander-in-chief of the army, the President of the United States used a different flag on land. This was also blue with many white stars within its angles and a large crimson

introduced in 1690 by Denmark. This had a white square placed in the centre, charged at first with the royal cipher and later with the whole achievement of the royal arms. This model became standard in Scandinavia and was later copied by many other countries.

The third model was adopted by Napoleon I, who in 1804 placed the state arms in gold in the centre of the French *Tricolore*, on which golden bees were scattered. This flag was again in use from 1852 to 1870, and since 1871 the French presidents have placed their ciphers in the centre. The first to add an additional device (the cross of Lorraine) was Charles de Gaulle. From 1974 to 1995 the French presidential flag was charged with the presidential emblem instead of a cipher.

◆ **ABOVE**
Royal flag of Poland (1605). Personal flag of King Sigismund III.

◆ **FAR RIGHT ABOVE**
Flag of the Duke of Anhalt (1815–1918).

◆ **FAR RIGHT BELOW**
Presidential flag of Germany (1919–1921).

star in the centre, heavily outlined in white and defaced with the state coat of arms.

A variation of the second model was the field striped in the livery colours and/or swallow-tailed. Such, for example, were the Polish royal flags of the three kings from the Vasa dynasty (1587–1668).

The third model appeared next. The arms are displayed in the centre of a national flag or war ensign. The first of such flags was the war ensign

FRENCH PRESIDENTIAL FLAGS

ALBERT LEBRUN (1932–1940)

HENRI PHILIPPE PÉTAIN (1940–1945)

CHARLES DE GAULLE (1958–1969)

GEORGES POMPIDOU (1969–1974)

VALÉRY GISCARD D'ESTAING (1974–1981)

FRANÇOIS MITTERAND (1985–1995)

The first major modification of the second model of the flag of a head of state was accomplished in 1828 when Austria changed the design of its imperial banner. A border in livery colours composed of white, red, yellow and black triangles was added to the yellow square field and the state arms were placed in the centre. This design was copied by Brunswick (1831–84), Bavaria and several other countries after World War I so it may be considered to be the fourth model.

Elaborate personal flags were introduced in 1844 in Prussia for the king, the queen and the crown prince and, although slightly modified in 1858 and 1889, they survived until 1918. Three elements of the design – the cross, the arms encircled with the collar of an order and the emblems in the corners – influenced not only the imperial flags of Germany but also the flags of other rulers. A very similar flag with a cross and three crowns in each corner was adopted by the grand duke of Oldeburg. The flag of the grand duke of Baden had a cross but the emblems in the corners were omitted. The royal flag of Italy, adopted in 1880, followed the Prussian design to some extent. The arms were placed in the centre of a square field and encircled with the collar of the Order of the Annunciation, and in each corner appeared a representation of the royal crown. Thus the fifth model of a royal or presidential flag was established.

FLAGS OF RULERS AND PRESIDENTS FOLLOWING THE AUSTRIAN DESIGN

EMPEROR OF AUSTRIA (1828–1894)

EMPEROR OF AUSTRIA – HUNGARY (1894–1915)

KING OF BULGARIA (1908–1918)

KING OF BULGARIA (1918–1947)

PRESIDENT OF CZECHOSLOVAKIA (1920–1939 AND 1945–1960)

PRESIDENT OF POLAND (1928–1945)

CHIEF OF THE HUNGARIAN STATE (1938–1945)

KING OF ROMANIA (1938–1947)

PRESIDENT OF SLOVAKIA (1939–1945)

CHIEF OF STATE OF CROATIA (1941–1945)

◆ **RIGHT**
King of Prussia's standard (1889–1918). Drawing by Hugo S. Ströhl.

◆ **FAR RIGHT**
Crown prince of Prussia's standard (1889–1918).

◆ **BELOW RIGHT**
Empress of Prussia's standard (1889–1918).

◆ **BELOW**
German imperial flags:
(first row) 1871–1890: emperor's standard, empress' standard, crown prince's standard; (second row) 1890–1918: emperor's standard, empress' standard, crown prince's standard.

◆ **ABOVE**
Flag of the king of Italy
(1880–1946).

◆ **RIGHT**
Flag of the German chief
of state (Adolf Hitler)
(1935–1945).

◆ **TOP**
Flag of the king of Württemberg
(1884–1918).

◆ **ABOVE**
Egypt, royal naval flag (1923–1952).

◆ **LEFT**
Presidential flag of the United States
(1888–1945).

Tunis combined emblems from the Turkish
military flags with stripes in colours
characteristic of the flags of North Africa. The
King of Siam chose a blue field with a red
border, charged with a combination of the
attributes of his royal and military authority
and the coat of arms.

In some countries, including Prussia and
Germany, there were separate flags for the ruler's
wife and for the crown prince. Some monarchies
also had flags for the queen mother and other

When in 1916 the President of the United
States decided to have just one flag for use both
on land and at sea, he added a white star to each
corner of his naval flag. This inspired several
countries in Latin America and the Philippines
to adopt similar flags. The American presidential
flag was modified again in 1945, the four stars
in the corners being replaced by a ring of
48 white stars (one for each state) encircling the
coat of arms. The number of stars was increased
to 49 in 1959 (for Alaska), and to 50 in 1960

members of the royal family. In the last quarter
of the 19th century, for example, Russia had
five flags and five broad pennants for the
members of the imperial family: empress,
crown prince, crown princess, grand duke,
grand duchess.

(for Hawaii). The only country that has
followed suit is the Philippines.

The models established in Europe for the
flags of heads of state were widely copied in the
Americas and partly in Africa and Asia. Some
rulers, however, adopted flags of a quite different
design. The King of Annam followed the
pattern of the Chinese flags, while the Bey of

CURRENT PRESIDENTIAL AND ROYAL FLAGS

Contemporary presidential and royal flags are presented in this section in chronological order according to the appearance of each model of flag. The oldest model, the armorial banner, has been used as a personal flag without interruption only by the rulers of Great Britain. Since 1837 the British royal banner has been quarterly England (first and fourth quarters), Scotland (second quarter) and Ireland (third quarter). There are separate armorial banners for the Duke of Edinburgh, the Queen Mother, the Prince of Wales, Princess Margaret and the other members of the Royal Family. The last of these, identical to the royal banner with a border of ermine, made history when it covered the coffin of Princess Diana.

Queen Elizabeth II also has special royal banners when she visits her ex-dominions such as Canada, Australia, New Zealand and Jamaica, or other monarchies of which she is the head of state. If she is visiting a country for which no special banner has been designed, she uses her personal flag which is a blue fringed field with the initial "E" in gold and ensigned with the royal crown, all within a chaplet of golden roses. This flag was used for the first time during the Queen's visit to India in 1961.

Remarkably, armorial banners are used as the flags of heads of state not only in European countries with a long heraldic tradition, such as Norway and Ireland, but in countries where this

tradition is quite recent or non-existent. The oldest example is the royal banner of Tonga, introduced in 1862; another is the royal banner of Thailand, adopted in 1917, which displays the mythical Garuda, the bird of the god Vishnu. The banners of the presidents of Gabon and Guyana are fairly recent; the first was designed by Louis Mühlemann, the famous Swiss heraldist and vexillologist, the second by the College of Arms in London.

The largest group of current royal and presidential flags has a unicolour field charged with the arms or emblem, and in a few cases

◆ **ABOVE**
Royal banner of Great Britain (since 1837).

◆ **LEFT**
Royal flag of Tonga (since 1862).

◆ **LEFT**
Royal flag of Norway (since 1905).

◆ **FAR LEFT**
Personal flag of Queen Elizabeth II.

displaying another device such as the party emblem (Kenya) or an inscription (Bangladesh, Kazakhstan, Malawi). The colour of the field is usually one of the colours of the national flag. Several presidential flags displaying the arms in the centre of a unicoloured field have a border of one to three colours. In the Czech Republic the border is patterned on the Austrian version.

There are several ways to deface a national flag with the arms or a presidential emblem.

They are usually positioned in the centre of the flag but sometimes appear in the upper hoist (Egypt, Finland, Morocco, Turkey), centre hoist (Eritrea, Namibia), top centre (Kuwait, Swaziland) or lower hoist (Saudi Arabia). In a few cases the emblem replaces the one on the national flag (Eritrea, Maldives, Pakistan).

The fifth, and last, model survived mainly in countries that copied the American flag. For example, the presidential flag of Cuba has been modified to display six stars instead of four, and in the Peruvian flag the stars have been replaced by yellow suns.

These five models inspired the designs of almost all the flags adopted before World War II. Another model was added when the French colonies gained independence. This is the simplest model, a square and fringed variant of the national flag, used in some former French colonies south of the Sahara, and in Tunisia and Syria.

Several flags of heads of state defy classification. Their designs combine features of the first and fourth models (Slovakia), the second, fourth and fifth (Sri Lanka) or the third

◆ ABOVE
(left to right)
Presidential flag of Israel (since 1948); presidential flag of Germany (since 1950); presidential flag of Italy (since 1990); presidential flag of Slovenia (since 1995).

◆ LEFT
Presidential flag of the Czech Republic (since 1993).

and fourth (Liechtenstein). The presidential flag of India looks heraldic but instead of heraldic figures it displays: the whole state arms (first quarter); an elephant symbolizing patience and strength (second quarter); scales representing justice and thrift (third quarter); a vase of lotus flowers representing prosperity and wealth (fourth quarter). The royal flag of the Netherlands is the only flag to have a cross as

◆ FAR LEFT TOP
Presidential flag of Iceland (since 1944).

◆ FAR LEFT CENTRE
Presidential flag of Finland (since 1978).

◆ FAR LEFT BOTTOM
Royal flag of Denmark (since 1972).

◆ LEFT
Presidential flag of Russia (since 1994).

◆ **LEFT**
Presidential flag of the
United States (since 1960).

◆ **RIGHT**
Royal flag of the Netherlands
(since 1908).

◆ **LEFT**
Presidential flag of Ghana
(since 1960).

◆ **BELOW LEFT TOP**
Presidential flag of South
Korea (since 1967).

◆ **BELOW LEFT CENTRE**
Presidential flag of India
(since 1950).

◆ **BELOW LEFT BOTTOM**
Royal flag of Jordan
(since 1928).

an additional charge. Around the arms is a ribbon with the insignia of the most distinguished Dutch military decoration, the Order of William.

Many countries do not have a special flag for the head of state, including the sixteen monarchies under Queen Elizabeth II of Great Britain. Some one-party countries do not have presidential flags for political reasons and a few simply do not see the need for a special flag.

THE BASIC MODELS OF CURRENT HEAD OF STATE FLAGS

An armorial banner is used in:
GABON, GREAT BRITAIN, GUYANA,
IRELAND, NORWAY, THAILAND, TONGA.

A unicolour flag defaced with the arms
or an emblem is used in:
BANGLADESH, BOTSWANA, BRAZIL,
BRUNEI, DOMINICA, GREECE,
INDONESIA, JAPAN, KAZAKHSTAN,
KENYA, KOREA, LUXEMBOURG,
MALAWI, MALAYSIA, MONACO,
MOZAMBIQUE, PHILIPPINES,
PORTUGAL, SINGAPORE, SPAIN,
TRINIDAD AND TOBAGO, UNITED
STATES, URUGUAY, ZAMBIA.

A national flag or ensign defaced with
the arms or an emblem is used in:
AUSTRIA, BELARUS, CHILE, DENMARK,
EGYPT, ERITREA, FINLAND, FRANCE,
ICELAND, KUWAIT, MALDIVES, MOROCCO,
PAKISTAN, RUSSIA, SAUDI ARABIA,

SENEGAL, SEYCHELLES, SUDAN, SURINAM,
SWAZILAND, SWEDEN, TURKEY.

A flag with a border and defaced with
the arms or emblem is used in:
CZECH REPUBLIC, GERMANY, ISRAEL,
ITALY, NEPAL, SLOVENIA, TAIWAN,
TANZANIA.

A flag defaced with the state or royal
arms and with an emblem repeated in
all four corners or sides is used in:
ARGENTINA, BELGIUM, CUBA, LIBERIA,
MALTA, THE NETHERLANDS, PARAGUAY,
PERU, VENEZUELA.

The heads of state of the following
countries have flags that do not
conform to any of the models
described: CROATIA, DOMINICAN
REPUBLIC, INDIA, JORDAN, LIECHTENSTEIN,
NAMIBIA, SLOVAKIA, SRI LANKA, UGANDA.

Government Flags

As well as a national flag, over 20 nations also have a state flag for use by government authorities. In five Scandinavian countries the state flag is a swallow-tailed or triple swallow-tailed version of the national flag. The state flags of other countries are their national flags but with the addition of the state arms in the centre.

The United States has one flag for all purposes, but the federal government and military authorities use it only in the official proportions of 10:19, making it the de facto state flag. The same flag in different proportions (2:3, 3:5 and 5:8) is the national flag for other uses, including use by the general public. There are no international regulations pertaining to the use of foreign flags in a country hosting an international conference or officials from a foreign country. Normally state flags should

◆ **LEFT**
Denmark, state ensign (since 1907).

◆ **LEFT**
Iceland, state flag and ensign (since 1918).

be used but there are exceptions to this rule. At the United Nations headquarters in New York, although some countries (Austria, Denmark, Finland, Germany, Iceland, Monaco, Norway and Sweden) have both state and national flags, they choose to be represented by their national flag.

◆ **FAR LEFT TOP**
Germany, state flag (1893–1918).

◆ **FAR LEFT BOTTOM**
Germany, state ensign (1893–1918).

◆ **BELOW**
Mecklenburg, state flag (1900–1918).

GOVERNMENT DEPARTMENTS AND AGENCIES

The United States is the only country with special flags for all its government departments, and some government agencies. They are displayed at, or on, the buildings of the departments and in the offices of high-ranking officials. The oldest is the flag of the National Aeronautics and Space Administration (NASA), introduced in 1960. Other countries have only a few departmental flags: Russia instituted a flag for its Finance Ministry in 1902, and Denmark adopted a flag for its Naval Ministry in 1916.

Many countries have flags for members of the government. The idea of distinguishing important members of the imperial or royal household with flags probably originated in highly hierarchical societies such as China, Russia and Prussia. From China the custom spread to several countries in South-east Asia such as Kelantan, one of the member-states of Malaysia. In the 1930s Kelantan had seven flags for the members of the royal family and the titled members of the royal dynasty, nine for members of the government and eight for the chiefs of districts.

◆ **LEFT**
Hesse, state flag (1902–1918).

◆ **LEFT**
US Department of Treasury (since 1963).

◆ **BELOW**
Flags of Kelantan.

In monarchies, and also in some countries with a republican government, there were (and in a few instances still are) flags for the prime minister. In the past the prime ministers of Italy, Greece and South Africa had their own distinctive flags. Countries that still have a flag for the prime minister include Portugal, Spain, Japan, the Maldives, Thailand, the Bahamas, Barbados, Jamaica, Surinam, and Trinidad and Tobago. In most of Germany there are different flags for the members of the local government (prime minister, ministers, state secretaries, senators and council members).

In countries where government officials have their own flags, the most common examples are flags of the navy and defence (or war) ministers. These were first seen in Russia in 1827 and 1893 respectively, and since then more than 20 countries, mainly in Europe and the Americas, have adopted separate flags for their ministers. Portugal, the United States and Chile have separate flags for their defence minister and their navy minister. Spain, Austria, Thailand, Chile and Ecuador have a separate flag that can be used by other cabinet ministers.

◆ **BELOW**
Ministers' flags:
(*clockwise from top left*)
The Italian prime minister,
Benito Mussolini (1927–
1944); prime minister of
the Bahamas (since 1973);
Russian navy minister (1827–
1918); German defence
minister (1935–1945);
Spanish navy minister.

◆ **RIGHT**

Flags of ministers in the United States:
(*from left to right*) Secretary of State, under Secretary of State; secretary of war, assistant secretary of war; secretary of treasury, under secretary of treasury; assistant secretary of treasury, attorney general. Plate from the *Flaggenbuch*, 1939.

◆ **BELOW**

Current flags of ministers of defence: (*from top to bottom right*) Great Britain, France, The Netherlands, Italy, Slovenia, Saudi Arabia.

Vereinigte Staaten von Amerika

II

Flagge des Staatssekretärs
(Außenminister)

Flagge des Unterstaatssekretärs

Flagge des Kriegssekretärs

Flagge des Hilfskriegssekretärs

Flagge des Schatzsekretärs

Flagge des Unterschatzsekretärs

Flagge des Hilfsschatzsekretärs

Flagge des Generalstaatsanwalts

The most complete set of flags for government officials, as well as departments, is in the United States, where in all departments there are separate flags for the secretary, under-secretary and assistant secretary. The heads of

The Danish flag is the war ensign with a white crown in the canton; the government vessels of Fiji display the national flag with the field changed to dark blue. The field of the government vessels' flags in India and Sri Lanka

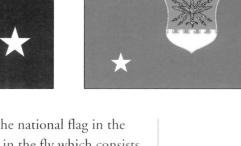

many government agencies and services also have their own distinguishing flags. The first to possess his own flag was the secretary of the navy in 1866, followed by the secretary of war in 1897.

In many countries government-owned vessels and vessels that provide services for the government do not fly the civil ensign. In New Zealand and Peru they hoist the national flag but in Argentina, the Dominican Republic, Ecuador, Haiti and Venezuela they hoist the state flag. Denmark, Belgium and some Commonwealth countries have special flags for government service vessels.

is also dark blue, with the national flag in the canton and an emblem in the fly which consists of a golden anchor and two crossed golden anchors, respectively. A few countries also have ensigns for vessels providing specialized services such as fishery control or lighthouse services.

GOVERNORS AND ENVOYS

The colonies of European powers were at first administered by the trade companies such as the East India Company, but in the 19th century this role was taken over by governors who acted as the representatives of the crown or government. Their flags followed the pattern of the national flag (Germany, the Netherlands, Spain, Belgium); displayed the national flag in the canton (France); or were charged with the state arms (Italy, Portugal).

Since 1891 the Italians had had a flag for their governors and in the 1930s they adopted a different one for the viceroy of Ethiopia which was white with a blue border, the state arms in the centre and yellow fasces in the corners. Portugal had three flags for its governors, all of which displayed the same emblem of the state arms on the cross of the Order of Christ. The flag of the Portuguese governor-

Governor of Belgian Congo.

general is illustrated; the flag of the governor had two vertical green stripes instead of horizontal ones; the flag of the governor of a district had one horizontal stripe.

Great Britain introduced two different flags for the representatives of the king or queen in its dominions and colonies. The flag of the governor-general of a dominion is dark blue, with the royal crest in the centre and the name of the dominion in a scroll beneath. A governor or lieutenant-governor uses the Union flag with a badge on a white disc surrounded by a garland of laurel superimposed on the centre of the flag. The last flag remains unchanged to this day but some of the governor-generals' flags have been diversified by the addition of local emblems such as a maple leaf (Canada), a whale's tooth (Fiji) and a two-headed frigate bird (Solomon Islands). In Canada the lieutenant-governors of the provinces have flags, of which only the flag of the lieutenant-governor of Nova Scotia follows the British pattern, with a garland of

Governor of German colonies.

Governor-general of Dutch colonies.

Governor of the Italian colonies.

Governor-general of Portuguese colonies.

Governor of French West Africa.

Governor of Surinam.

Governor-general of Australia (1902–1936).

Governor-general of Pakistan.

Governor-general of South East Asia.

Governor-general of the West Indies.

Governor-general of the Union of South Africa.

Governor-general of the Federation of Rhodesia and Nyasaland.

◆ ABOVE

Historic flags of governors.

Governor-general of Canada.

Governor-general of Fiji.

Governor-general of Solomon Islands.

Lieutenant-governor of Nova Scotia.

Lieutenant-governor of Quebec.

Lieutenant-governor of British Columbia.

Governor-general of Gibraltar.

Administrator of the French Southern and Antarctic Territory.

maple instead of laurel. The flags of other lieutenant-governors (except that of Quebec) have the same design as that of the lieutenant-governor of British Colombia.

A few countries have special flags for their diplomatic representatives. The first were introduced in Russia in 1833 for the ambassador or envoy extraordinary, consul-general, consul and chargé d'affaires or resident. The flag of the ambassador was in the form of the Russian jack, with the small imperial arms in the white canton. The national flag with the war ensign in the canton, served as the flag of the consul-general, and the flag of the consul was a swallow-tailed version of the consul-general flag. The flag of the chargé d'affaires or resident was white, with the war ensign in the canton. The

designs of these flags were changed in 1870, and again in 1896. Not many countries followed suit but among them were China, Italy and Thailand, which adopted their diplomatic flags at the end of the 19th century. In the 20th century the United States introduced a flag for consuls and flags for envoys were also introduced by Iran (the ambassador's flag and the flag of the envoy extraordinary), Egypt, Spain, Colombia and Mexico (the flag of the Diplomatic Corps and the Consular Corps).

Great Britain has two flags for its diplomats. The flag of an ambassador is the Union flag with the royal arms on a disc encircled by a garland of laurel superimposed in the centre. The consul's flag is identical except that it displays the royal crown instead of the arms.

◆ ABOVE
Current flags of governors.

POST, CUSTOMS AND COASTGUARD FLAGS

The first flag for customs vessels was introduced by Denmark in 1778. It was a specially marked Danish war ensign and was flown by vessels when hailing other ships in the course of duty. In 1793 Denmark adopted a similar flag for mail-carrying ships. At the end of the 18th century two other countries, Spain in 1793 and the United States in 1799, adopted flags for their customs vessels. It was prescribed that the American Revenue ensign, as it was called, would be used by cutters and boats employed in the service of the Revenue and would be "always displayed over the custom-houses of the United States, and over the buildings appertaining to the Treasury Department of the United States". The ensign, which underwent some minor alterations, is still in use today at sea.

Flags for both post and customs services were introduced by Great Britain in the early 19th century; by Russia in 1849 (post) and 1858 (customs); Prussia in 1863; and Norway in 1898. In this century both post and customs flags were adopted by the other Scandinavian countries, as well as by Thailand and Mexico. Currently customs flags are also used in Spain, Russia, Turkey, Brazil, China and Tonga.

France, the United States, Poland and a few other countries use a distinctive post flag. In some countries there are two post flags of different designs; one is flown from the post office's buildings, the other is flown from mail-carrying vessels.

In most countries the responsibility to guard territorial waters and fight against smugglers belongs to the navy and, indeed, it is the only task of the naval forces of most countries in the Caribbean, Africa and Oceania. In some countries, however, guarding the coastline is the

♦ **BELOW**
Current customs flags:
(*left to right*) Denmark, Great Britain, Russia, Turkey, China, United States, Mexico, Ukraine.

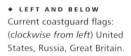

◆ LEFT AND BELOW
Current coastguard flags:
(*clockwise from left*) United States, Russia, Great Britain.

duty of a special force, the coastguard, which is not actually a part of the navy. The United States Coastguard has the longest-standing traditions. Their ensign was based on the revenue ensign flown on ships of the Revenue Cutter Service. The name "coastguard" was first used in 1915 when the Revenue Cutter Service merged with the Life-saving Service. The current United States Coastguard ensign was introduced in 1966 and a similar one with six vertical stripes was soon adopted by Haiti. Other countries that currently use a distinctive coastguard flag include Great Britain, Poland, Russia and Yugoslavia.

POLICE FLAGS

Only a few countries have police flags displayed at police stations or elsewhere outdoors. Generally they are of two types: a ceremonial flag made of expensive fabric with embroidered police badges, designed for the interior of the building, or a flag that resembles a military colour. In some countries there is also a distinguishing flag for police commandants, used both as a decoration of office and as a car flag.

The same devices appear regularly on police flags. A flaming grenade is an emblem that Napoleon I granted to his élite troops as a battle honour and it is now used as a police emblem in France, Belgium, the Netherlands and Italy. Another device is a silver (white) star with five to nine points made of different-length rays which is found on police emblems on all continents but mainly in Great Britain and Commonwealth countries, the United States and Germany. Police flags are flown on police stations in Great Britain, Turkey, Finland, Israel and Japan.

In France there is no police flag. The organization of the police resembles that of the military so there are regimental and battalion standards, in the same design as military colours. The units of the Gendarmerie Mobile and Gendarmerie Départementale have standards with their names in semi-circles above and below a flaming grenade, and the reverse bears a shield with the regional arms or the arms of the legion. Belgium also does not have a police flag but it has a flag for the commandant of gendarmerie, the commandants of the six regions, the commandants of the Mobile Legion and the Royal School of Gendarmerie. These are used in offices and as a car flags.

The Royal Canadian Mounted Police (RCMP) adopted its flag in 1991, together with flags for its divisions in all provinces and territories. All of them have a red field with a blue canton bordered with yellow and defaced with the badge of the RCMP. The flags of the divisions have an emblem in the lower hoist displaying the most characteristic figure from the arms of the province or territory.

In some countries there is a specialized harbour police. Its vessels fly distinctive ensigns, which generally consist of the national or war ensign charged with the police badge.

◆ **BELOW**
Police flags: *(clockwise from top left)* Finland, Turkey, Bermuda (central emblem), Brabant, *Gendarmerie mobile* standard (France).

Military Signs

The flag epitomizes for an army the high principles for which it strives in battle ... It keeps men's motives lofty even in mortal combat, making them forgetful of personal gain and of personal revenge, but eager for personal sacrifice in the cause of country they serve.

GILBERT GROSVENOR, *SPECIAL EDITION OF THE NATIONAL GEOGRAPHIC MAGAZINE "FLAGS OF THE WORLD"*, WASHINGTON, 1917.

We shall probably never know when and where vexilloids were first used in battle, but it is safe to guess that large groups of early warriors had signs to rally around and to follow. The oldest surviving vexilloids, from Egypt, follow definite patterns, suggesting that they had evolved from earlier models.

From earliest times a vexilloid or flag carried in battle had a semi-sacred quality. In the Middle Ages and subsequent centuries a new flag was consecrated before a battle and blessed by priests, and after the campaign it was kept in a local church. Mercenaries, and later the soldiers of standing armies, took a holy oath to defend their "colour" to the death. At the time of the crusades, banners with a cross prevailed, but soon armorial banners and pennons, standards and guidons were introduced. Many troops used banners with religious motifs, such as painted figures of the Virgin Mary and Child or various saints.

By the 16th century the banners carried by infantry had reached enormous dimensions, and in the cavalry a large swallow-tailed pennon was the most common form of flag. In the first half of the 17th century regiments began to wear uniforms, and the flags of both infantry and cavalry were therefore in the same colours. Military banners in France, Spain and England acquired marks of national identification: a white cross, the cross of Burgundy and the cross of St George, respectively.

Regulations adopted in the 18th century prescribed both the design and the number of colours in a regiment, and from then on the colour consisted of a staff with a finial and a flag. These three parts were inseparable and had to be treated as a simple unit; sometimes saving just the colour's finial from a battlefield saved the honour of the unit. Standardization gradually occurred in most countries, and more colours acquired national characters. The armed forces of many countries also adopted a wide range of other flags to distinguish the branches of the armed forces and the ranks of their commanders.

◆ **LEFT**
Banner of the Republic of Venice (15th century).

BATTLE BANNERS

In the Middle Ages five types of flag were used on a battlefield. Three of them (banner, pennon and pencel) bore the owners' arms, the other two (standard and guidon) were in the livery colours with badges. Most important was the banner representing the troops of the king, prince, duke, earl, baron or bishop, and the banners of the military orders. Royal banners are described in the chapter *Emperors, Sovereigns and Presidents*, but the flag of the Teutonic Order and some territorial flags are illustrated here. The pennon was the personal flag of a knight bachelor responsible for smaller formations of men. The pencel, or *pennoncelle*, was the personal flag of a knight, carried on a lance. The standard and the guidon were used by the infantry and cavalry, respectively, to identify bodies of troops within an army.

The 16th century witnessed an entirely new way of conducting warfare. In some countries, mainly the German states, mercenaries replaced troops in a province or country. The ruler contracted an experienced soldier to raise and lead a regiment of infantry and provided arms and flags for each company, with up to ten flags for the whole regiment. The design of these banners was usually based on multiple divisions of the field (horizontal, vertical, diagonal and combinations of these) and simple charges such as bend, cross or saltire and narrow wavy triangles. The banners were called *Landknechtsfahnen*, after the German word *Landknecht* (foot-soldier). The banners of these regiments became more elaborate in the 17th century, and regiments fighting on the Protestant side often displayed flags that insulted the

◆ **BELOW**
Territorial flags in the 14th century: *(from left to right)* Teutonic Order; Silesia; Pomerania; Bishopric of Warmia.

In contrast with the earlier simplicity, the armorial banners of the 15th century were made of costly materials decorated with rich embroidery. Heraldic figures became very ornate and battle banners with religious motifs gradually became more numerous, the most popular being the Virgin Mary and Child or Christ on the Cross. Spain, Austria and Bavaria used a border on their colours, which was not seen on the colours of Protestant countries. The custom of using religious motifs on military flags survived into the 20th century. The Virgin Mary appeared on Austrian colours until 1938; Christ's Passion was depicted on many Russian colours in the 19th century; St Andrew and his cross appeared on the Serbian colours carried in World War I and St George slaying the dragon was painted on the colours of the Greek Army.

◆ **BELOW**
(top) Bavarian infantry (17th century); *(bottom)* Polish cavalry (17th century).

Catholic Church and the clergy, or scenes from fables such as a bear with lambs or a fox with hens. Both sides began to use propaganda slogans and allegorical emblems such as the Roman goddesses Fortuna and Justice, an arm in armour emerging from a cloud, or a lion trampling a fallen warrior.

At the beginning of the 17th century the standing armies established permanent units divided into a regular number of companies, with a clear division between infantry and cavalry. Banners reached enormous sizes, exceeding the men's height. During the Thirty Years War (1618–1648) the company under the command of the colonel adopted a different-coloured flag to the other companies in the regiment. In most countries white was chosen for the field of the colonel's flag.

STANDARDIZATION OF COLOURS

Regimentation and standardization began early in the 17th century. The infantry regiments were divided into three wings, each with a distinctive flag. They began to display the colours of the uniforms, the wings being distinguished only by different heraldic badges or symbols. In some countries the colours bore national symbols such as the cross of St George or the cross of Burgundy, in which case they revealed country, regiment and battalion at a glance. A century later the number of wings was reduced to two and so there were only two colours. The first was generally called the "king's or sovereign's colour" and was a symbol of allegiance and service to monarch and country. It was borne by the first battalion, originally the colonel's battalion, and was therefore referred to as the "colonel's colour". The second was known as the "battalion colour" ("regimental colour" in Great Britain and the United States) and represented the honour and traditions of the regiment and the soldier's duty to the regiment.

The first national symbol to appear on military flags was the red cross of Burgundy, introduced in 1516 as the main device of the flags of the Spanish infantry. Under a decree of 1707, each battalion had three colours, and the 1st Battalion carried the colonel's colour, white, with the cross of Burgundy and badges between

◆ **ABOVE**
Spanish colours: (*from the top*) Regimental infantry banner (1550); colonel's infantry colour (1707); regimental infantry colour (1775); colonel's infantry colour (1802–1931).

◆ **ABOVE AND LEFT**
French colours: (*above*) Regiment of Picardy (1597); (*left*) infantry colour (1812).

its arms. The regimental colours had fields in the regiment's facing colours or in the principal colour of the coat of arms from the place where the regiment was formed; a badge and the name of the unit were in the centre. In the late 16th century the fields of some flags became multicoloured, borders were added, and some fields and borders displayed very intricate designs. A decree of 1728 introduced a new model of the colonel's colour and provided each battalion with two colours: the 1st Battalion having the colonel's colour and one battalion colour, both white. The battalion colour had the cross of Burgundy with a badge at each end, while the colonel's colour displayed the royal arms with the Order of the Golden Fleece and the provincial arms in each corner. On the reverse the arms were placed on the cross of Burgundy with the provincial arms at each end, and were supported by two red lions. In 1808 the number of colours was reduced to one per battalion: the 1st Battalion used the king's colour in the same design as the previous colonel's colour, and the battalion colour remained unchanged.

The next to standardize their battle flags were the French in 1597. The flags were square, with a width exceeding 180 cm (6 ft). They were divided by a white cross and the four parts of the field displayed the regimental colours. The first four permanent regiments were assigned the following colours: red (Picardy), green (Champagne), gold (Navarre) and black (Piedmont). The colours of the other regiments had fields in two or three colours. Borders and simple devices (squares, fleurs-de-lis, crowns) or mottoes were added, but the basic design survived until 1794. In 1804 Napoleon I introduced the famous "eagles", named after the finial in the form of an eagle of ancient Rome. The plinth on which the eagle stood bore metal numerals indicating the regiment to which the colour belonged. The design was changed in 1812, and again in 1815. The French pattern of colours was adopted by Italy, and in the 20th century by many countries in Europe and elsewhere.

◆ **ABOVE**
Prussian colours (*from left to right*) Infantry colour (1701–1729); infantry colour (late 18th century).

The first colours of the Prussian infantry, introduced in 1701, had a central oval emblem containing the Prussian eagle encircled by a wreath and ensigned with the royal crown, with the royal ciphers in the corners. There were two flags for each battalion. The first flag of the 1st Battalion was called the *Leibfahne*, the second the *Regimentsfahne*. The 2nd battalion had two *Regimentsfahnen* in the same design but with the

colours interchanged. The *Leibfahne* had the centre in the regiment's colour and the field in the same colour as the centre of the *Regimentsfahne*. In 1729 a cross was added to the field, which was either wavy or straight. The Prussian design was followed by Baden, Brunswick and Hesse during the Napoleonic Wars, and by Saxony (1735–1810), Russia (1800–57), Bavaria (1841–1918) and Poland (1919).

The first standardization of Russian military flags was carried out in 1712, when the infantry and dragoon regiments obtained flags in the same design. Usually the fields were unicolours, some with simple divisions or charges such as a cross or saltire. The regimental emblem appeared in the upper hoist, with the heraldic charge of the province or town after which the regiment was named. In 1727 the colonel's

◆ **RIGHT**
German colours in 1910. Plate from the *Fahnen und Standartenträger*.

Bild: 7
Fahne vom I. Bataillon des 8. thür. Infanterie-Rgts. Nr. 153 Sachsen-Altenburg 1910

Bild: 8
Fahne vom I. Bataillon des 7. thür. Infanterie-Rgts. Nr. 96 Reuß j. L. 1910

Bild: 9
Fahne vom III. Bataillon des 7. thür. Infanterie-Rgts. Nr. 96 Schwarzburg-Rudolstadt 1910

Bild: 10
Fahne vom anhaltschen Infanterie-Rgt. Nr. 93, 1910

Bild: 11
Fahne vom braunschweig. Infanterie-Rgt. Nr. 92, 1910

Bild: 12
Fahne vom großherzogl.-oldenburg. Infanterie-Rgt. Nr. 91, 1910

colour in both the infantry and cavalry attained national character. It was white, with a large representation of the imperial arms, and the company and squadron flags had fields in the regiment's facing colour, with a border of triangles. The emblem was the crowned imperial cipher encircled by a wreath, underneath which was a scroll with the regiment's name. Each infantry regiment received a colonel's colour and six company colours, and each dragoon regiment received a colonel's colour and eight squadron guidons. Under Catherine the Great the design of the Russian colours gradually changed until in 1800 it was nearly identical to that of Prussia. Further minimal changes took place in 1803 and 1813. After 1813 the colours of the line infantry were green with white corners; the colours of the guard infantry had the same design, but with yellow fields and corners in different colours.

The first detailed regulations governing the design of British colours were issued in 1747 and reduced the number of flags to two per battalion of the line infantry. The first was the King's colour, i.e. the Union flag with the regimental badge in the centre. Badges recalling service overseas were the green dragon (China), the sphinx (Egypt), the tiger (Bengal) and the elephant (India), and each badge was encircled by a wreath of roses (England) and thistles (Scotland). The other flag was the regimental colour, usually in the regimental facing colour with a small Union flag in the canton and the same badges as on the king's colour. In 1801 the Irish cross of St Patrick was added to the Union flag and the shamrock to the wreath.

The common element of the colours of Swiss regiments in foreign services were the "flammes", long wavy triangles radiating in all directions from the centre to the edges of the field. They were mostly in the livery colours of the regimental owners or commanders. This design was created at the end of the 17th century as the ordnance flag of regiments in service to the king of France and it was later introduced by other Swiss troops in service in the Netherlands, Spain, Venice, England and Naples.

In 1796 the United States Army introduced colours for the infantry. The national colour was blue with a representation of the national arms (in many artistic variations) in gold, and a golden scroll with the name of the regiment; the regimental colours were white or yellow. Very similar colours were used by the cavalry until 1895. In 1841 the infantry were given entirely different colours resembling the national flag.

◆ **ABOVE**
Austrian colours:
(*left*) Regimental colour
(1806–1815);
(*right*) infantry colour
(1915–1918).

◆ **FAR LEFT**
Battalion colour of the
Cisalpine Republic.

◆ **LEFT**
Polish legion in Lombardy.
Colour of the 1st Battalion
of Riflemen.

appeared in the centre of the company's colour and in the upper hoist of the king's colour. In the kingdom of Hanover, where the same custom applied, the provincial arms were placed in the corners of the military colours. Similarily, the colours of the Spanish infantry bore the provincial arms in all four corners, and the arms of the province encircled by a wreath was the central device for the Finnish colours during World War II.

◆ **ABOVE AND LEFT**
(*clockwise from far left*)
Colours of Swiss troops in foreign services: Spain, France, Great Britain, Holy See.

  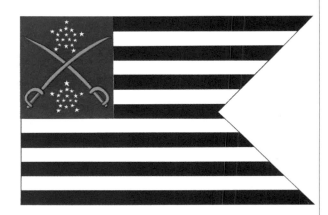

The arrangement of the stars on the new colours varied considerably, as did their colour (white, yellow or gold) and number of points. During the Civil War the Southern armies' battle flag and colours were based on the national flag's design, with inscriptions identifying the regiment and places of victorious battles.

As well as the national symbol, many of the colours used by different armies also carry symbols of the province of the regiment's origin. In Sweden, where regiments were named after provinces, the arms of the province

◆ **ABOVE**
Colours of the United States: (*left to right*) Infantry colour (1841 model); artillery regimental colour (Civil War period); first cavalry division (Civil War period).

◆ **LEFT**
Battle flag of the Confederacy States of America (1861–1865).

BATTLE HONOURS

◆ LEFT
Battle awards in the form of streamers: (*left*) the 3rd Infantry Regiment of Württemberg; (*right*) the 1st Regiment of Saxon Grenadiers (c.1900).

In ancient Rome the military standards, or vexilloids, of the bravest troops were augmented with battle honours, in the form of crowns, wreaths, medals or rings attached to the staff. In modern times there have been several methods of distinguishing a military colour with battle honours: an inscription sewn or painted on the field; a ring attached to the staff; a streamer with metal plates or with embroidered or painted inscriptions; or the order, or other decoration, pinned to the flag or the cravat.

In modern times, the custom first developed in the Prussian Army at the beginning of the 18th century. The awards took the form of a ribbon with a small metal plate, tied to the top of the staff. In 1785 three regiments of the Army of Hanover received the first honours in the form of golden embroidered inscriptions.

In the French Army the first battle honours were added to the colours in 1791. After 1808 the honours were restricted to major victories where Napoleon commanded in person: Ulm, Austerlitz, Jena, Eylau, Friedland, Eckmühl, Essling and Wagram, Marengo and Moscowa (Moscow). In Britain the practice of naming the places of great victories on the colours themselves was sanctioned in 1811. After 1844 the addition of battle honours was allowed only for the regimental colour. The most often awarded honours were for the Battle of Waterloo and the Peninsula war.

In the United States Army awards were inscribed on flags long before the first regulation allowed this in 1862. During the Civil War the first battle honour appeared in the form of streamers with inscriptions. This practice was supported by many, both military and civilians, who believed that nothing should be allowed to mar the stripes of the national flag. This sentiment grew and in 1890 the United States Army decided to use awards in the form of silver rings or bands only, and in 1920 they were replaced with streamers. The Marine Corps followed suit in 1939, the Air Force in 1956, the Coastguard in 1968 and the Navy in 1971. Today the honours earned by a unit are displayed as streamers attached to the staff of the unit's battle and organizational colour. There are fewer than ten award streamers (commendations and presidential citations) but over 100 campaign streamers.

◆ BELOW
Current colours: (*from left to right*) Germany, Poland, Portugal.

FLAGS OF ARMED FORCES

Many flags have been designed since World War II for use at ceremonies and parades as well as inside offices or headquarters buildings. At least three countries have a special flag for their armed forces as a whole. The flag of the British Joint Services, introduced in 1964, is composed of three vertical stripes of dark blue (the Royal Navy), red (the Army) and light blue (the Royal Air Force). In the centre is a black emblem: a foul anchor for the Navy, two swords for the Army and an eagle for the Air Force. A similar emblem designed for the Canadian armed forces in 1968 is blue on the white field of the Canadian forces ensign, which also serves as the naval jack. China has a flag for use by its Army, Navy and Air Force. It resembles the national flag but instead

♦ **ABOVE LEFT**
Canadian forces ensign.

♦ **ABOVE RIGHT**
Chinese armed forces flag.

♦ **RIGHT**
Poland: (*from top to bottom*) Branches of the armed forces since 1993: Army, Navy, Air Force.

♦ **ABOVE AND RIGHT**
United States: (*clockwise from top left*) Army (since 1956); Navy (since 1959); Marine Corps (since 1956); Air Force (since 1952); Coastguard (since 1964).

of stars has stylized characters for "8" and "1" to commemorate the date of the foundation of the People's Liberation Army, 1 August 1928.

A few countries have flags for each branch of the armed forces. The United States and South Korea also have a flag for their Marine Corps, and the United States has a fifth flag for its Coastguard. In 1962 the United States Army field flag was introduced. It is the same design as the army flag with an ultramarine blue field, the army emblem (without the Roman numerals) in white and a white scroll inscribed in scarlet. Others authorized to use this flag include separate brigades such as divisions, numbered commands,

◆ **ABOVE**
Israel: (*from left to right*)
Army, Navy, Air Force.

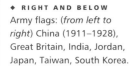
◆ **RIGHT AND BELOW**
Army flags: (*from left to right*) China (1911–1928),
Great Britain, India, Jordan,
Japan, Taiwan, South Korea.

general officer commands, headquarters of the United States Army garrisons, missions, recruiting main stations and the regional headquarters of the Reserve Officers' Training Corps.

A set of flags for the Polish armed forces was introduced in 1993; their main characteristic was uniform shape and colour. The fields are defaced with representations of the metal cap badges of each branch of the armed forces. The flags of the three branches of the armed forces in Israel have either the national flag in the canton or the flag design on the field. They also have distinctive finials in the same shape as the emblem on the particular flag.

The first army flag was probably the Chinese one, introduced in 1911. Great Britain also chose red for the background of its army flag, adopted in 1938, with the royal crest on two crossed swords. A similar flag was adopted for the Army of Independent India. The army flags of Colombia and Indonesia have a unicoloured field defaced with the army emblem, and the army flags of Japan and Taiwan are variations of the national flag. In other countries the army uses the national flag with an emblem in the centre (Thailand) or in the upper hoist (such as the two crossed sabres of Egypt or the army emblem of Kuwait).

AIR FORCE FLAGS

Air force flags are flown on land at airfields and where units are stationed. They are also hoisted on a small staff over an aircraft when VIPs are embarking or disembarking.

The first flag for use by the aeronautic division of the army was introduced in Russia at the end of the 19th century. It was similar to many flags used by the navy, a white field with the jack in the canton but with the centre of the fly defaced with the aeronautical emblem in red. The British Air Force flag, introduced in 1918, was patterned on the navy ensigns but with light blue for the field. This colour and the design of the British Air Force flag have been adopted by many countries.

Many countries adopted air force flags with the light blue field but without the canton. Zambia has a roundel in the centre, while Japan, South Korea, Taiwan, Indonesia,

◆ **BELOW**
Air force flags:
(*from left to right*)
United Kingdom, Colombia,
India, Sri Lanka, Malaysia,
Belgium, Taiwan, Poland.

the Philippines and Colombia have the air force emblem in the centre. Belgium positioned the air force emblem in the upper hoist and the roundel in the centre, and Kuwait positioned the emblem in the centre and the roundel in the upper hoist. The air force flag of the Netherlands is blue with an orange pile charged with a flying eagle under a crown. The design of the Israeli Air Force's flag resembles the national flag but the shield of David is solid. The flag of the Australian Air Force is a light blue version of the national flag, with the roundel in the lower hoist.

The fields of the air force flags of Spain, Poland and Thailand consist of the national flag. The air force emblem appears in the centre of the top stripe (Spain) or in the centre (Thailand). The Spanish flag also displays the state arms in the centre.

AIR FORCE FLAGS OF THE BRITISH MODEL

The air force flags of the following countries have a light blue field, a canton with the national flag and the air force roundel in the fly:
CANADA, COLOMBIA, EGYPT, GHANA, GREAT BRITAIN, INDIA, JORDAN, KENYA, MALAYSIA, MYANMAR, NEW ZEALAND, OMAN, PAKISTAN, SAUDI ARABIA, SINGAPORE, SRI LANKA, SUDAN.

DISTINGUISHING FLAGS

In most republican countries the head of state is also the commander-in-chief of the armed forces, so there are no special flags for the commander-in-chief. In monarchies such flags are also very rare, although Sweden has such a flag. In some countries there are separate flags for the commanders-in-chief of the army and navy.

Distinguishing flags of chiefs of staff are more common. In Great Britain and Italy the chiefs of the defence staffs have flags, as do the chiefs of

◆ ABOVE, LEFT AND BELOW
Flags of chiefs of staff: Great Britain, chief of defence staff; France, chief of general staff; Italy, chief of defence staff.

the general staff or the chiefs of the staff of the army and/or the air force in many other countries.

The largest set of these flags is in the United States, where the armed forces use many distinguishing flags. For example, the Army's own flags are adjutant general, chief of the army reserve, judge advocate general, chief of chaplains, chief of the national guard bureau, chief of engineers, surgeon general and inspector general.

◆ FAR LEFT
The flag of the commander-in-chief of the armed forces, Sweden.

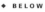

◆ BELOW
Flags of the chiefs of staffs in the United States: (*left*) Joint chiefs of staff chairman; (*right*) joint chiefs of staff vice-chairman.

The rank flags of the United States Army correspond with those of the Navy, but the Army uses red for the field colour.

There are also rank flags for the National Guard, blue with the crest of the individual State Army National Guard. The lieutenant-general's flag has three white stars, one on each side of the crest and one above the crest. Two other flags have the crest in the centre of the field: the flag of the major general has one star on each side of the crest; the brigadier general's flag has one star above the crest.

◆ **ABOVE AND RIGHT**
Rank flags in the United States Army: (*clockwise from far left*) General of the army, general, lieutenant general, major general, brigadier general.

◆ **ABOVE**
Rank flags in the British Royal Air Force: (*from left to right*) Marshal, air marshal, air vice-marshal, air commodore.

◆ **RIGHT**
Flag of the lieutenant general of the National Guard in New Mexico.

Naval Ensigns and Flags

At sea, flags became a necessity from the first time a ship ventured out of its home waters. Wherever men have sailed on the oceans their flags have indicated their nationality and allegiance and the ship without a flag has justly been recognized in international law as a pirate.

WHITNEY SMITH, *THE FLAGBOOK OF THE UNITED STATES*, NEW YORK, 1970

The main flag on a ship of war is the war ensign, which identifies its nationality; the jack has a similar function to this. Rank flags and commission pennants indicate the rank of the ship's commander.

For centuries most flags were designed for use at sea rather than on land. The first markings of ownership and nationality were emblems (and later coats of arms) painted on a ship's sails; shields attached along the gunwales served a similar function. When flags were gradually introduced in the 12th and the 13th centuries they became an indispensable means of identifying the nationality and function of a ship, and the rank of its commander.

Until the 13th century naval activity was local and temporary. All ships were armed to some degree but there was no distinction between merchant and naval ships. To denote nationality, most ships flew the flag of their home port. The first national flags used by ships seem to have been the English cross of St George and the Danish *dannebrog* in northern Europe; the Genoese cross of St George and the Venetian lion of St Mark in the Mediterranean region.

◆ **BELOW**
(from left to right) English red ensign (1653–1801); English white ensign (1653–1702); English blue ensign (1653–1801); English white ensign (1702–1801); Denmark (since 1625).

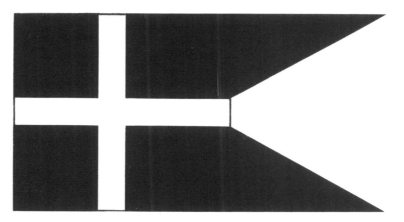

WAR ENSIGNS THROUGH HISTORY

The first navy, equipped with well-armed fighting ships, was organized in England in the first half of the 16th century. Under Elizabeth I (1558–1603) it developed into a major defence force and later played a decisive role in the extension of the British Empire. In Elizabethan times each English ship of war

◆ **BELOW**
(*from left to right*)
Sweden (1663–1815 and since 1906); Sweden (1844–1905); Sweden (1815–1844).

The design of the British ensigns with the Union Jack in the canton had a great impact on the war ensigns of many other European countries. France adopted a similar ensign in 1790, adding a canton displaying the jack in republican colours to the white field of the ensign used in times of monarchy. The next

flew a different striped ensign, but the device common to all of them was the cross of St George in the canton. The stripes, mostly horizontal, varied in number (from five to eleven) and colouring (red, white; green, white; red, white, blue; red, green, red, blue, and so on). In 1625 the British Navy was divided into three squadrons, each of which was given an ensign in a different colour. Red was assigned to the centre, commanded by the admiral of the fleet; blue to the van, commanded by the vice-admiral, and white to the rear, commanded by the rear-admiral. This division was abolished in 1864, leaving only the white war ensign. The blue ensign became the ensign of the Royal Naval Reserve and could also be used by the officers of the Reserve when they commanded a private vessel. Currently, the criteria for warrants to wear the blue ensign, laid down in the Queen's Regulations of 1983, are:

The officer commanding a ship other than a fishing vessel must be an officer on the Retired or Emergency Lists of the Royal Navy or a Commonwealth Navy, or an officer on the Active or Retired Lists of any branch of the Reserves of such navies. If the rank held on one of these Lists by the officer commanding the ship is below that of Commander, at least one other officer in the ship's company must be an officer on one of the Lists mentioned.

◆ **RIGHT**
Sardinia (1815–1848).

◆ **RIGHT**
France (1790–1794).

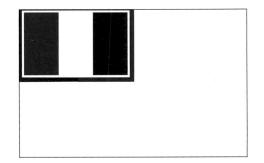

◆ **RIGHT**
Confederate States of America (1863–1865).

countries to follow suit were Sweden and Sardinia in 1815, and in 1844 the Swedish jack was changed to display the colours of the flags of Sweden and Norway. The jack, in a square form, was used in the canton of the white war ensign of the Confederate States of America.

Prussia (1819–1850).

Germany (1867–1892).

Germany (1892–1903).

Germany (1903–1919).

Spain (1785–1931).

Austria (1787–1915).

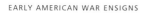

Russia (c.1700–1918 and since 1992).

Soviet Union (1924–1935).

EARLY AMERICAN WAR ENSIGNS

War ensign of the ship *Serapis* (1779).

Ensign from the Lotter flag chart (1793).

War ensign from the Scotti flag chart (1796).

Ensign from a Swedish flag chart (1805).

In the 18th and 19th centuries another popular model for a war ensign was the Dutch ensign, with horizontal stripes. In 1701 Prussia introduced a plain white ensign charged with the small arms and the Iron cross. The Spanish ensign, adapted in 1785, displayed livery colours defaced with the state arms. The stripes of the Austrian war ensign, adopted in 1787, were of the same width, charged with the crowned shield of the historic arms.

The united Germany settled on a design combining a Scandinavian cross with a jack in the canton and a small state arms displayed on a white disc in the centre of the cross. There were minor subsequent changes to this design.

The American war ensign was presumably intended to be identical to the national flag but most of the actual ensigns show the stripes in three colours, which conform to the descriptions given by American diplomats in response to questions from European governments. Replying to the kingdom of Naples, Benjamin Franklin and John Adams wrote, "the flag of the United States of America consists of thirteen stripes, alternately red, white and blue". American ensigns with stripes in these three colours are depicted in many British, German, French, Italian and Swedish almanacs, and in flag charts dating from the late 18th and early 19th centuries. It seems that ensigns with three colours of stripes and those with red and white stripes were in use simultaneously. Paintings of ships in John Paul Jones's squadron by a Dutch artist show the ensign of *Serapis* with blue, red and white stripes and the ensign of *Alliance* with red and white stripes.

One of the oldest war ensigns still in existence today is the Russian one, adopted in about 1700 by Peter the Great for his navy, which displays a blue St Andrew's cross on a white field. As in Great Britain, this ensign was assigned to the centre, commanded by the admiral of the fleet; blue and red ensigns with a blue saltire in a white canton were assigned to the van and the rear respectively. Since 1865 the sole war ensign has been the white one.

WORLD WAR II

Among the major nations taking part in World War II only Italy, Japan, the United States, Great Britain and France used the same war ensign that they had used during World War I, which had ended some 21 years earlier. Similarly, most of the ensigns used in World War II are now obsolete; the war ensigns of Japan, Great Britain and France are the only exceptions. Indeed, France's ensign has remained the same since 1853, Great Britain's since 1864 and Japan's since 1889. The war ensign of Poland has now

Germany (1937–1945).

Japan (since 1889).

Italy (1848–1945).

The Norwegian Hirdmarinen.

Croatia (1941–1945).

Romania (1921–1948).

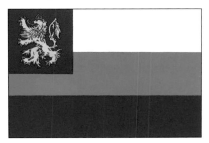
Bulgaria (1928–1947).

only slightly different arms to the World War II version, and the ensign of the United States now has two more stars in the canton. The war ensign of China did not change, but it is now used by Taiwan.

Two war ensigns were also used on land. The war ensign of Nazi Germany was also the

flag of the armed forces, and the ensign of the United States was traditionally both the national flag and the ensign.

The Norwegian Hirdmarinen, illustrated here, which was formed by the Quisling regime in 1942 was intended mainly to train recruits for the German Navy.

◆ **ABOVE**
War ensigns of the Axis countries.

◆ **BELOW**
War ensigns of the Allied countries.

Poland (1928–1945).

United States (1912–1959).

United Kingdom (since 1864).

Egypt (1923–1958).

France (since 1853).

Soviet Union (1935–1992).

CURRENT WAR ENSIGNS

Most of the countries that became independent after World War II adopted national flags for general use on land and at sea, i.e. the national flag also served as the war ensign. Almost all of the countries that have adopted distinctive war ensigns were part of the British Empire and most of them followed the example of the British white ensign. The war ensigns of the Bahamas, Ghana, India, Jamaica, Nigeria and the Solomon Islands are white with the red cross of St George and a national flag in the canton. The war ensigns of Bangladesh, Kenya, Malaysia and Singapore are white with the national flag in the canton and in some a badge in the fly, while the ensigns of Australia, Fiji and New Zealand are variations of the national flag and have a white field. Two other war ensigns,

those of Tonga and Ukraine, are clearly based on the British white ensign.

Fewer than 40 countries of the world have war ensigns that differ from their national flags, and in several other cases the war ensign has the same design as the national flag but in different proportions. The ensigns of Grenada, Guyana, Pakistan, and Trinidad and Tobago have overall proportions 1:2 and each stripe of the French has a different width (90, 99 and 111 units when the width of the ensign is 200 units).

The ensigns of the Scandinavian countries, Germany, Poland and Estonia are swallow-tailed and triple swallow-tailed, following the custom that evolved centuries ago in the Baltic Sea region. The Finnish ensign was adopted in 1918 and the current pattern was introduced in 1978,

♦ **FAR LEFT**
India (since 1950).

♦ **LEFT**
Tonga (since 1985).

♦ **FAR LEFT**
Ukraine (since 1997).

♦ **LEFT**
Australia (since 1967).

♦ **FAR LEFT**
New Zealand (since 1968).

♦ **LEFT**
Malaysia (since 1968).

◆ RIGHT
Germany (since 1956).

◆ FAR RIGHT
Finland (since 1978).

when the shape of the arms and the shade of blue were changed slightly.

The war ensigns of other countries are either variations of the national flag (Thailand, Egypt, Saudi Arabia and Bulgaria) or have totally different designs in national colours (Israel, South Korea and Belgium).

Generally the war ensign is worn by naval ships and by vessels that provide services to the navy. In some countries there are special ensigns for auxiliary vessels: the Royal Fleet Auxiliary Service has the British blue ensign charged with a yellow anchor, and the Russian auxiliaries fly a dark blue flag with the war ensign in the canton.

◆ RIGHT
Thailand (since 1917).

◆ FAR RIGHT
Israel (since 1948).

◆ RIGHT
South Korea (since 1949).

◆ FAR RIGHT
Belgium (since 1950).

◆ RIGHT
Pakistan (since 1956).

◆ FAR RIGHT
Egypt (since 1973).

THE JACK

The second flag denoting the nationality of a naval vessel is a flag hoisted from the jackstaff, the top mast on the bow. The jack is usually square and is flown exclusively by ships in harbour or when the ship lies in the roadstead.

Most of the early jacks were identical with the flag used at sea by merchant and naval ships. The first English flag, white with the red cross of St George, was used as the jack of ships of war until 1606 and as the jack of merchant ships until the middle of the 19th century. Like the ensign, it influenced the design of jacks in other European countries and in America. The first to borrow the English design, in reversed colours, was Peter the Great, Tsar of Russia, followed by the Baltic States, which began to organize their navies after World War I. The British jack with a cross and saltire inspired the Dutch to divide the field gyronny in their national colours.

Several jacks are based on armorial banners. Spain has such a long tradition of using armorial banners at sea that it is not surprising that its

◆ LEFT
Great Britain (1606–1801).

current jack displays the arms of Castile, León, Aragon and Navarre. The first Italian jack displayed the cross of Savoy; the present one, adopted in 1954, displays the Venetian lion of St Mark and the crosses of the ancient maritime republics Genoa, Amalfi and Pisa. The Croatian jack of 1941–1945 was an armorial banner, charged with the badge of the ruling Ustasha.

Other jacks bear the state arms or emblem as the charge. The shield of the Portuguese arms is

Russia (c.1700–1920 and since 1992).

Bulgaria.

Latvia.

Estonia.

The Netherlands (since the end of the 17th century).

Paraguay (since 1934).

Germany (1867–1919).

Soviet Union (1924–1935).

Sweden-Norway (1844–1905).

Norway (since 1905).

Confederate States of America (1863–1865).

♦ RIGHT
(*clockwise from left to right*):
Germany (1921–1933);
Thailand (since 1917);
Soviet Union (1932–1992).

Italy (since 1954).

Finland (since 1978).

placed on an armillary sphere (a navigational instrument in the Age of Discovery). State arms have also appeared on the jacks of Finland, Romania, Persia (Iran) and Peru. A few jacks have white stars on a dark blue field; the Chilean jack has one star, while the jacks of Brazil and the United States display as many stars as they have states (currently 27 and 50 respectively). The second jack of the Soviet Union displayed the main communist emblems from the arms and national flag, the red star and the hammer and sickle.

The last group of jacks are the national flag defaced with an emblem. The German jack, for example, was defaced with the Iron cross and the jack of Thailand with the navy's emblem. In many countries the war ensign takes the place of a distinctive jack (Denmark, Sweden, France, Germany and South Korea), in others it is the same as the national flag (Turkey, Bangladesh,

Japan, Australia, New Zealand, Mexico, Dominican Republic, Colombia and Ecuador) or a square version of the national flag (Belgium). The jack often has the design of the canton of the national flag (Great Britain, Greece, Taiwan, Chile and the United States). In some countries in Latin America it has the design of a historic revolutionary flag (Cuba, Mexico and Uruguay).

Portugal (since 1910).

Taiwan (since 1949), (China 1912–1949).

Italy (1879–1946).

Argentina (since the end of the 19th century).

Spain (since 1945).

United States (since 1960).

Philippines (since 1955).

Croatia (1941–1945).

RANK FLAGS

In a few countries there are distinguishing flags for the commander-in-chief of the navy and the chief of staff of the navy. The predecessors of these flags were admiralty flags, adopted in the early 18th century by the Boards of the Admiralty in Great Britain and Russia. The admiralty managed naval affairs and also functioned as an operational authority, and its prerogatives were transferred in time to the navy or defence department.

In Norway, Finland and Ukraine the commanders-in-chief of the navy use war ensigns with emblems in the canton: a white saltire, a blue anchor over crossed yellow cannons and three stars respectively. The flag of the commander of the Russian Navy is the war ensign with the state arms on a disc surrounded by a garland of laurel. The flags of the chiefs of naval staff in France and Thailand are the national flag with an emblem in the centre.

Distinguishing flags are quite recent but the system of identifying the rank of ships' commanders is more than 400 years old. The English Navy was divided in 1545 into the van, the centre and the wing. The lord admiral (commander of the centre) flew the royal banner at the main and the flag of St George at the fore; the admiral of the van squadron flew the flag of St George at the main and fore; and the admiral of the wing squadron flew the flag of St George at the mizzen and bonaventure mizzen. The fleet sent to attack Cadiz in 1596 was divided into

♦ **ABOVE**
Flags of the commander-in-chief of the navy:
(*top*) Portugal,
(*bottom*) Ukraine.

♦ **ABOVE LEFT**
British Admiralty.

♦ **LEFT**
Russian Admiralty.

♦ **ABOVE**
Flags of the chiefs of staffs of the navy:
(*top*) France, (*middle*) Italy, (*bottom*) Russia.

four squadrons, each with three flag officers. The admiral's command flag was flown at the main, a vice-admiral's at the fore and a rear-admiral's at the mizzen. This system of identifying ranks was retained after the restoration of the monarchy, when there were only three squadrons – red, blue and white. The admiral of the fleet, commanding the red squadron, flew the Union flag at the main, unless he was the lord high admiral and was entitled to fly the royal standard. The vice-admiral and rear-admiral of the red squadron flew plain red flags on the fore and mizzen respectively; the admirals, vice-admirals and rear-admirals of the blue and white squadrons flew plain blue or white flags at the main, fore and mizzen respectively. This system was copied by fleets in other European countries and survived to the 19th century, when it became impractical because of changes in ships' architecture. Command flags of different designs for each flag officer were introduced at this point instead.

Throughout history there have been four basic methods of distinguishing rank among flag officers: (i) the same flag at different mastheads; (ii) the same design in different colours; (iii) the same basic design charged with additional devices for the lower ranks, and (iv) the same basic design charged with additional devices, the number of which increases with the rank. All four methods were employed in the United States Navy from 1817 to 1876. The order of colours denoting seniority was established in 1817. It was used in the Navy until 1870 and is still valid for distinguishing the flags of secretaries, deputy secretaries and under-secretaries in government departments.

Today the first two methods of distinguishing rank are obsolete. The only exceptions to this are the rank flags in the Yugoslav and French navies, which follow the second method. In France an admiral uses the national flag with four blue stars in the centre, and a vice-admiral displays three white stars in the upper hoist of the national flag. A rear-admiral uses the national flag, but with an additional white horizontal stripe of the same width as the vertical one and two white stars in the upper hoist. The third method is used only in the navies of Germany, Great Britain, Greece, Japan and Portugal; all other countries use the fourth method. Five-pointed stars are mostly used but other devices include circles (as in the case of Great Britain, Germany, Portugal, Spain and Colombia); six-pointed stars (the Netherlands); horizontal stripes (Japan and Taiwan), and suns (Peru). The field of a rank flag is generally unicoloured, mostly blue, and occasionally the field is charged with a cross (Great Britain, Germany, Portugal and Colombia) or other device (Japan). In some countries the field has the design of the war ensign (Denmark, Norway and Sweden), the national flag (the Netherlands, Spain, Romania and Mexico) or has adopted the design of its canton (Greece).

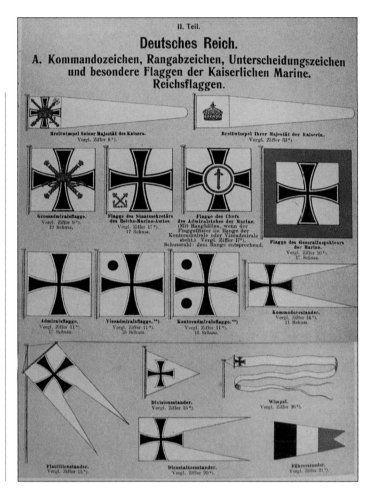

◆ LEFT
Distinguishing and rank flags in the German Navy. Plate from the *Flaggenbuch*, 1905. The rank flags are still in use.

◆ BELOW
Rank and other naval flags as presented in the *National Geographic* in 1917.

CURRENT RANK FLAGS

GREAT BRITAIN

ADMIRAL

VICE-ADMIRAL

REAR ADMIRAL

NORWAY

ADMIRAL OF THE FLEET

ADMIRAL

VICE-ADMIRAL

REAR ADMIRAL

THE NETHERLANDS

ADMIRAL

ADMIRAL LIEUTENANT

VICE-ADMIRAL

REAR ADMIRAL

YUGOSLAVIA

ADMIRAL OF THE FLEET

ADMIRAL

VICE-ADMIRAL

REAR ADMIRAL

UNITED STATES

ADMIRAL OF THE FLEET

ADMIRAL

VICE-ADMIRAL

REAR ADMIRAL

TURKEY

ADMIRAL OF THE FLEET

ADMIRAL

VICE-ADMIRAL

REAR ADMIRAL

SAUDI ARABIA

ADMIRAL

VICE-ADMIRAL

REAR ADMIRAL

COMMISSION PENNANTS

In the 13th century it was the custom to attach long streamers to the mastheads of ships purely for decoration, and four centuries later it became a duty of all men-of-war to fly a masthead pennant to distinguish them from merchant ships. Until the late 19th century each English or Russian warship used a pennant of its squadronal colour, either red, white or blue. Today there is only one commission pennant for all naval vessels, which should fly continuously day and night during the period the ship is in commission. If the ship is commanded by a flag officer, the appropriate rank flag replaces the commission pennant. The commission pennant is the longest, but narrowest, flag on a ship. Its width is 6–20 cm (2½–8 in) and its length 15–50 times greater. The largest pennant used during World War II by German warships was 20 cm (8 in) wide and 16 m (17½ yd) long. Most commission pennants copy the design of the national flag or display the national flag in the hoist. Some arrange the national colours differently or display in the hoist only the main design element from the national flag or war ensign.

Sweden (1815–1844).

Sweden (since 1906).

Great Britain.

France.

Japan.

Italy.

Finland.

Turkey.

Sweden (1844–1905).

United States.

Russia.

Germany.

The Netherlands.

Norway.

Spain.

Ukraine.

Flag Families

Flags are a universal characteristic of human civilization. With the exception of the most primitive societies and nomadic peoples, it appears that every culture has invented for itself flags of one kind or another – with a remarkable similarity of form observable throughout the world. The functions of flags are nearly identical in all societies, and parallels in flag usages may be observed in diverse regions and eras.

So strong is the tradition of flags, we may not be far from the truth in surmising that there is a law – not of nature, but of human society – which impels man to make and use flags. There is perhaps no more striking demonstration of this than the fact that, despite the absence of any international regulation or treaty requiring of a national flag, without exception every country has adopted at least one.

WHITNEY SMITH, *FLAGS THROUGH THE AGES AND ACROSS THE WORLD*, 1975.

In the Middle Ages flags on land denoted mainly rulers and the military, but at sea they were used to denote nationality. With the growth of international trade in the 17th and 18th centuries, more countries began to adopt merchant ensigns and these became well known not only in their home ports but also inland. Thus in most countries with access to the sea the merchant ensign, or a flag similar to it, eventually became the national flag.

Looking at the various flags hoisted at the UN headquarters in New York, at the NATO headquarters in Brussels or at stadiums during international sporting events, we may wonder why the flags of nations in different parts of the world have such similar designs. In most cases the similarity is deliberate. It may be an expression of common history, traditions or interests, or it may be a statement that a country modelling its flag on that of another country sees that country as a religious or political role model.

The similarity of flags is as old as the use of flags themselves, but flag use did not develop on a large scale until the 19th century and continued during the 20th. Out of some 195 independent countries only 12 have flags whose designs were adopted before 1800. Seven of

these (Denmark, Great Britain, the Netherlands, Russia, the United States, France and Turkey) have influenced the designs and colours of over 130 national flags and ensigns, which are grouped into ten large and three smaller "flag families". Some flags may belong to more than one flag family, for example flags displaying the pan-Arab colours and the Muslim crescent, or those displaying the French colours and the cross.

◆ **BELOW**
Flags at the Rockefeller Center in New York, 1968, show the similarities between many flags.

THE CHRISTIAN CROSS

The cross is an ancient magical sign and decorative motif known in many parts of the world, such as Mesopotamia, China, Scandinavia and Greece, but today it is universally recognized as the symbol of Christianity. In the first centuries after the death of Christ the main Christian symbol was a fish, often with the Greek word IXΞYΣ (fish). This can be made into an acrostic: I (I) = Ieus, X (Ch) = Christos, Ξ (Th) = Theou, Y (U) = Uios, Σ (S) = Soter, meaning "Jesus Christ God's Son Saviour". In the 3rd century Christian communities began to use cross-like emblems, such as an anchor with a crosspiece or a human figure with outstretched arms. A breakthrough came in 326 when St Helena, mother of Emperor Constantine, was said to have discovered the cross on which Christ was crucified. This stimulated an increase in the devotion of the faithful and led to the cross being gradually introduced as a symbol of martyrdom, resurrection, redemption and salvation.

From the 9th century to the end of the 12th century a metal cross on the top of a mast was the only device marking

◆ **BELOW**
(from left to right)
Portugal (1140–1185);
Jerusalem; Genoa;
Constantinople (14th century);
Barcelona (14th century);
Sardinia (14th century);
Savoy (14th century).

merchant ships in northern Europe. Later the cross became the most common charge of the merchant ensigns of cities and countries in both Northern and southern Europe, for example Cologne, Riga, Elbing, Danzig, Königsberg, Geneva and Marseilles.

The oldest flags with a cross are those of Portugal and the kingdom of Jerusalem. From 1140 to 1185 the Portuguese flag was white with a blue cross on a white field, and from 1185 to 1250 it was white with a cross made of five blue shields; this latter arrangement remains to this day in the centre of the coat of arms of Portugal. The flag of the kingdom of Jerusalem under King Amalrich (1162–1173) displayed five golden yellow crosses on a white field.

Other flags and ensigns dating from the 13th and 14th centuries are charged with a simple

THE CROSS

The current national flags of the following countries and territories belong to this family:
ÅLAND ISLANDS, DENMARK, DOMINICA, DOMINICAN REPUBLIC, FAROES, FINLAND, GUERNSEY, ICELAND, JERSEY, MADEIRA, MARTINIQUE, NORWAY, SHETLAND, SWEDEN, SWITZERLAND, TONGA, WALLIS AND FUTUNA ISLANDS.

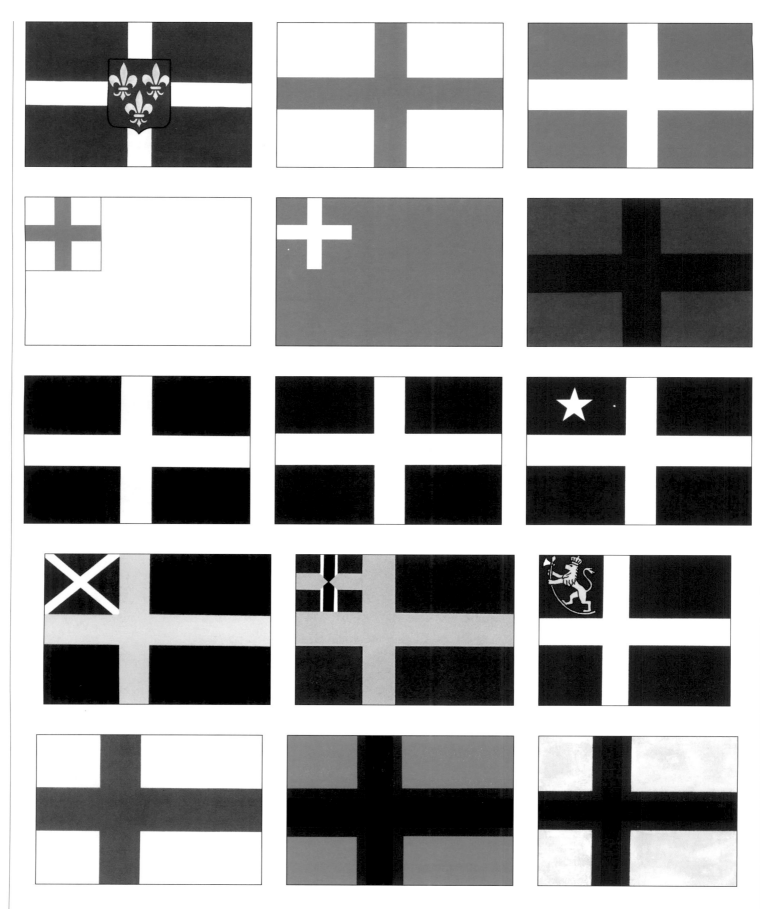

cross including the Teutonic Order, England, France, Denmark, Savoy and Malta, and the flags of Barcelona and Constantinople, which display additional devices. The flag of Barcelona has two quarters with the cross and two

displaying the armorial banner of Catalonia. The flag of Constantinople has four letters "B" between the arms of the cross, which are believed to stand for the Greek motto *Basileis Basileon Basileion Basileisi* ("King of Kings ruling

◆ **ABOVE**
(left to right from top left)
Switzerland, civil ensign (since 1941); Livorno; Malta (civil ensign since 1965); Samoa (1873–1885); Rimatara (c.1856–1891); Tongatapu (c.1858–1862).

◆ **OPPOSITE**
(left to right from top left)
France civil ensign (1661–1790); Provence; Calai;, Picardy; Marseilles; Oldenburg (1774–1935); Greece, national flag (1822–1970); Samos (1832–1913); Crete (1898–1913); Sweden, civil ensign (1815–1844); Sweden, civil ensign (1844–1905); Norway, civil ensign (1814–1818); Finland, civil ensign (since 1918); East Karelia (1920–1922); Ingermanland.

over Kings"). It inspired the flags adopted in subsequent centuries by at least two other countries in the Mediterranean: in the Sardinian flag there are Moorish heads between the arms of the cross, and in the Savoy flag the letters "FERT" stand for *Fortitudo Ejus Rhodum Tenuit* (His Courage Saved Rhodes).

In the 17th and 18th centuries the cross was the main charge of the civil ensign of France, and of several French provinces (Provence and Picardy) and ports (Marseilles and Calais). The official French civil ensign was blue with a white cross, with the royal arms overall, but it was not popular and most French merchant vessels used either provincial or port ensigns or the banned white ensign. Such widespread use of the cross in the Mediterranean also influenced the flags of nations created in the 19th and 20th centuries such as Greece, Samos and Crete.

Until the end of the 14th century the centre of the cross corresponded with the centre of the field. Denmark was the first to position the cross in such a way that the parts of the field between the arms of the cross formed squares in the hoist and rectangles in the fly. This example was followed by Sweden (1569), Norway (1821), Iceland (1915), Finland (1918), the Faroes (1919), East Karelia (1920), and Ingermanland and the Åland Islands (1921). Thus a large sub-family, called the Scandinavian cross, came into being. Modern flags with the Scandinavian Cross are illustrated in *Flags of Europe*.

As well as simple symmetrical or Latin crosses, there were some more elaborate versions of the Christian cross. One of the first, a red Maltese cross on a white field, is known from the war ensign of the Cavalieri di Santo Stefano Order, founded in 1561. A modification of this cross appeared in the 17th and 18th centuries on the merchant ensign of Livorno.

Four very old crosses have only appeared on civil ensigns and flags during the last 100 years. In Switzerland a white cross on a red field had already appeared in the 13th century on the flag of Schwyz and on red schwenkels added to the flags of other cantons. However, it did not become the national symbol until 1889 (national flag) or for use at sea until 1941 (civil ensign). The 900-year-old white Maltese cross of the Order of the Knights of St John of Jerusalem appears on the red field of the civil ensign of Malta. Finally the cross of the Portuguese Order of Christ, founded in the early 14th century, became the central emblem on the flag of Madeira in 1978.

In various forms, the Christian cross also appears on the flags and ensigns of nations in other parts of the world. It is a charge of the flags of Dominica and the Dominican Republic, and it was placed in the canton of the Liberian flag of 1827–47. In Oceania it was the charge of the civil ensigns of Samoa, Rimatara and Tongatapu, and it is still used by Tonga and by Wallis and Futuna.

THE MUSLIM CRESCENT

The crescent is one of the oldest symbols known to humanity. Together with the sun, it appeared on Akkadian seals as early as 2300 BC and from at least the second millennium BC it was the symbol of the Mesopotamian moon gods Nanna in Sumer and Sin in Babylonia, Sin being the "Lamp of Heaven and Earth". The crescent was well known in the Middle East and was transplanted by the Phoenicians in the 8th century as far as Carthage (now in Tunisia). In the 12th century it was adopted by the Turks and since then the crescent, often accompanied by a star and mentioned in the 53rd *surah* (chapter) of the Koran, has been the main symbol of Islam.

THE FLAG FAMILY

The current national flags of the following countries and territories belong to this family: ALGERIA, ANJOUAN, AZAD KASHMIR, AZERBAIJAN, BRUNEI, COMOROS, MALAYSIA, MALDIVES, MAURITANIA, NORTHERN CYPRUS, PAKISTAN, SINGAPORE, TUNISIA, TURKEY, TURKMENISTAN, UZBEKISTAN, WESTERN SAHARA.

The oldest representations of flags with the crescent are on 14th-century navigational charts, or *portolanos*, and the manuscript of a Franciscan friar. There are discrepancies between these sources as far as the colours of fields or

◆ **LEFT**
(left to right from top left)
Gabes; Tlemcen; Tunis; Turkey (16th–18th century); Turkey (1793–1844); Egypt (1914–1922).

THE UNION JACK

Until the early 17th century and since the 13th century the English flag and jack, used by both merchant and navy ships, had been white with the red cross of St George. The Scottish flag was blue with the white cross of St Andrew. Then, on 12 April 1606 King James I of England and Scotland issued a proclamation:

That from henceforth all our Subjects of this Isle and Kingdome of Great Britaine, and the members thereof, shall beare in their Maintoppe the Red Crosse, commonly called S. Georges Crosse, and the White Crosse, commonly called S. Andrewes Crosse, joyned together, according to a forme made by our Heralds...

This was the birth certificate of what soon became the best-known flag in the world.

Until 1634 the flag was used by both merchant and navy ships, thereafter its use was restricted to the king's own ships or ships in the king's immediate service; English merchant ships reverted to flying the St George's cross and Scottish ships the St Andrew's cross. At the same time the merchant ensign, red with the St George's cross in the canton, came into use and was later legalized in a proclamation of 1674. This proclamation retained the "Flag and Jack White, with a Red Cross (commonly called Saint George's Cross)", and repeatedly warned that use of the Union Jack was illegal. Nevertheless, many merchant captains

GENEALOGY OF THE UNION JACK

ST GEORGE'S CROSS   ST ANDREW'S CROSS   ST PATRICK'S CROSS

UNION FLAG 1606–1801

UNION FLAG SINCE 1801

continued to use the "King's jack" in order to gain advantages such as better protection, exemption from port duties in France as well as exemption from the requirement to use a pilot in Holland.

When the United Kingdom of Great Britain and Ireland came into existence on 1 January 1801, a red saltire called the cross of St Patrick was chosen to represent Ireland. It originated in the coat of arms of the Anglo-Irish family of Fitzgerald and was the main emblem of the Order of St Patrick, adopted in 1783. The idea of counterchanging the white and red saltires assured almost equal status for both of them, and was excellent from an artistic point of view. The new Union flag replaced that of 1606 in the cantons of the merchant ensign, and the red, white and blue ensigns used by the three squadrons of the Navy. On 9 July 1864 an Admiralty order abolished the division of the Navy into squadrons and assigned the white ensign exclusively to the Royal Naval Service, while the red ensign became "the national

colours for all British ships". It was decided that the blue ensign would

> be carried by all vessels employed in the service of any public office; by vessels employed under the Transport Department, and the Civil Departments of the Navy (with the Seal or Badge of the office to which they belong at the present), and, under our permission, by ships commanded by Officers of the Royal Naval Reserve Force...

The use of the blue ensign was extended by the Colonial Defence Act of 1865, which allowed "all vessels belonging to, or permanently in, the service of the Colonies" to use this ensign, "with the Seal or Badge of the Colony in the Fly thereof". This Act made possible the enormous future growth in the number of flags with the Union Jack in the canton. More than 100 colonial ensigns have been in use during the last century and some of them, such as those of Australia, New Zealand, Fiji and Tuvalu, became

◆ **BELOW**
(from left to right) Grenada (1903–1967); Nyasaland (1914–1953); Tanganyika (1919–1964); Gilbert and Ellice Islands (1937–1979); Burma (1939–1941); Sarawak (1947–1963); Federation of Rhodesia and Nyasaland (1954–1963); Guyana (1954–1966); Solomon Islands (1956–1977); Seychelles (1961–1976); the Bahamas (1964–1973); Dominica (1965–1978).

after some alteration the national flags of independent countries.

Formally the civil ensign of a British colony was always, and still is, an undefaced red ensign. Only a few dominions and one colony obtained the right to use the British red ensign defaced with a badge. The privilege was first granted to Canada (1892), then to New Zealand (1899), Australia (1903), South Africa (1910), Bermuda (1915), the Isle of Man (1971), Guernsey (1985), the Cayman Islands (1988) and Gibraltar (1996). The charges on the last two flags mentioned are of ancient origin. The golden cross on the civil ensign of Guernsey was the main charge of William the Conqueror's gonfanon, accorded to him by the Pope before he embarked on the campaign that ended in victory at the battle of Hastings in 1066. The ensign of Gibraltar

◆ **BELOW**
(from left to right)
Canada (1922–1957),
Canada (1957–1965),
Union of South Africa
(1912–1928).

displays the arms granted by King Ferdinand and Queen Isabella of Spain on 10 July 1502. Several former British colonies were so accustomed to the red ensign that after gaining independence they introduced a civil ensign in the form of a red flag with the national flag in the canton. As well as the examples illustrated here,

the civil ensigns of Sri Lanka, Bangladesh and the Solomon Islands also have this design.

The British innovation of putting the national flag in the canton of a flag or ensign greatly influenced the merchant ensigns of many countries that did not have formal ties with the British Empire. The example of the striped Elizabethan

♦ **OPPOSITE**
Badges of the British Colonies from *Flags of Maritime Nations*, 1914.

♦ **LEFT AND BELOW**
(left to right from top left)
Hanover (1801–1866);
Helgoland (1814–1890);
Australia, civil ensign (since 1908).
New Zealand, civil ensign (since 1903).
Singapore, state ensign (since 1966).
Isle of Man, civil ensign (since 1971).
Bahamas, civil ensign (since 1973).
Guernsey, civil ensign (since 1985).
Gibraltar, civil ensign (since 1996)

GREAT BRITAIN
COLONIES (CONTINUED)

TASMANIA

SOLOMON
ISLANDS

FIJI
ISLANDS

TERRITORY
OF PAPUA

BRITISH RESIDENT,
GILBERT & ELLIS ISLANDS

WESTERN PACIFIC
HIGH COMMISSIONERS

AFRICA

BRITISH CENTRAL AFRICA

BRITISH EAST AFRICA

SAMOLILAND

UNION OF SOUTH AFRICA

SIERRA LEONE

GOLD COAST

GAMBIA

CHINA

ST. HELENA

NIGERIA

UGANDA

HONG KONG

WEIHAIWEI

EAST INDIES

CEYLON

MAURITIAS

STRAITS SETTLEMENTS

SEYCHELLES

ensigns induced the Portuguese to adopt a similar ensign in 1640. The blue and red ensigns served as models for the civil ensigns or national flags of Hanover (1801–1866), Sardinia (1821–1848), Greece (1822–1828), China (1928–1949), Taiwan (since 1949), Spanish Morocco (1937–1956), Samoa (1948–1949), the Khmer Republic (1970–1975), and flags of the French colonies (see *The French Tricolore*).

The flag of the United States, a discussion of which follows, was one of the first flags to be modelled on the British ensign.

◆ **ABOVE AND LEFT**
(left to right from top left)
Burma (1948–1974);
Ceylon (1954–1972);
India, civil ensign
(since 1950); Pakistan,
civil ensign (since 1958);
Ghana, civil ensign
(since 1961); Greece,
civil ensign (1822–1828);
Taiwan, civil ensign
(since 1949); Spanish
Morocco (1937–1956).

THE FLAG FAMILY

The current national flags of the following countries and territories belong to this family:

ANGUILLA, AUSTRALIA, BERMUDA, BRITISH ANTARCTIC TERRITORY, BRITISH INDIAN OCEAN TERRITORY, BRITISH VIRGIN ISLANDS, CAYMAN ISLANDS, COOK ISLANDS, FALKLANDS, FIJI, HEBRIDES, MONTSERRAT, MYANMAR, NEW ZEALAND, NIUE, PITCAIRN, ST HELENA, SAMOA, SOUTH GEORGIA AND SOUTH SANDWICH ISLANDS, TAIWAN, TONGA, TURKS AND CAICOS ISLANDS, TUVALU.

THE STARS AND STRIPES

From the end of the 15th century North America was colonized by British settlers and the best-known flag was the British red ensign, which in America was used also on land. It was only natural that it should influence the design of the United States flag, often called the Stars and Stripes or Star-spangled Banner.

The first American flag was the merchant ensign, introduced in 1775. It consisted solely of 13 red and white stripes, very similar to the flag of the Revolutionary Society of the Sons of Liberty. The flag hoisted on 2 January 1776 by the Continental Army also had 13 red and white stripes, with the Union Jack in the canton. Called the Grand Union flag or the Continental Colors, it was identical to the flag of the British East India Company although this was probably just coincidence. The Union Jack in the canton symbolized continuing loyalty to Britain, but the stripes were probably taken from the merchant ensign rather than from the flag of the East India Company and symbolized the rebellion of the 13 colonies against British rule.

Some circumstances indicate that the Union Jack had already been replaced by the star-filled canton in 1776, and that the Continental Congress's Resolution of 14 June 1777 only confirmed the design already in use. Substantiating this theory is the terse wording of the Resolution:

Resolved, That the Flag of the United States be 13 stripes alternate red and white, that the Union be 13 stars white in a blue field representing a new constellation.

There is no mention of the size of the Union (the canton) or the shape or configuration of the stars. In fact, from that date there were two different designs for the canton of the American national flag. The so-called Betsy Ross design has the stars arranged in a circle, while Francis Hopkinson's design shows the stars arranged in parallel staggered rows. In both cases the stars were five-pointed, which was a revolutionary innovation in flag design.

◆ **RIGHT**
Grand Union flag.

◆ **RIGHT**
Betsy Ross design.

◆ **RIGHT**
Francis Hopkinson's design.

One of the earliest accounts of the symbolism of the flag is by Alfred B. Street, who in October 1777 witnessed the flag at the surrender of the British General Burgoyne at Saratoga:

The stars were disposed in a circle, symbolizing the perpetuity of the Union; the ring, like the circling serpent of the Egyptians, signifying eternity. The thirteen stripes showed with the stars the number of the United Colonies, and denoted the subordination of the States to the Union, as well as equality among themselves.

The growth of the Union posed the question of how the new states should be represented in the flag. After the admission of Vermont (1791) and Kentucky (1792) to the Union, the flag

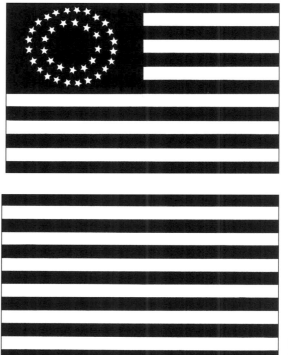

◆ **LEFT**
(from left to right)
Stars forming rings; stars forming ovals; stars forming a star; an early civil ensign.

created on 13 January 1794 displayed fifteen stars and 15 stripes. Between 1796 and 1817 five more states joined the Union but the flag was not modified until 4 April 1818, when the Flag Act raised the number of stars to 20 and reverted the number of stripes to the original 13. Section 2 of the act established the principle for future modifications:

And be it further enacted, that on the admission of every new State into the Union, one star be added to the union of the flag; such addition shall take effect on the fourth of July next succeeding such admission.

Since then the number of stars in the canton of the national flag has been increased 24 times, the latest being on 4 July 1960. From 1818 to this day the number of stars represents the

number of states in the Union, while the 13 stripes symbolize the 13 colonies that achieved independence and formed the United States of America.

For more than 130 years there was no official regulation of the arrangement of the stars in the canton of the national flag. At any given time the flags displayed dozens of designs, the most popular were concentric rings, ovals, diamonds and large stars made of smaller stars. Then, in 1818, President Monroe stipulated that the stars should be arranged in parallel rows. This arrangement was followed by the navy and was officially adopted for all flags in 1912.

THE FLAG FAMILY

The current national flags of the following countries and territories belong to this family:
ABKHAZIA, CHILE, CUBA, GREECE, LIBERIA, MALAYSIA, PUERTO RICO, TOGO, UNITED STATES, URUGUAY.

◆ **BELOW**
Flag with 48 stars (1912–1959).

The first country to adopt a similar flag to the American one was Hawaii. In an astute political move, the Hawaiian king combined in his country's flag the symbols of the two most influential powers in the Pacific, that is the British Union Jack with the tricolour stripes of the American ensign. Other countries adopted flags inspired by the American design to manifest their adherence to republican ideals of liberty and democracy. These countries included Chile (1817), Uruguay (1828), Texas (1836),

Vermont (1837), Cuba (1850), the Confederate States of America (1861), Louisiana (1861) and Puerto Rico (1891). Alternatively, some countries used the stars and/or stripes to represent the number of their subdivisions: Greece (1822); Liberia (1827); El Salvador (1865); Brazil (1889) and seven of its states (Amazonas, Bahia, Goiás, Maranhão, Piauí, São Paulo, Sergipe); as well as North Caucasia (1918); the Federation of Malaya (1950), Togo (1960) and Abkhasia (1992).

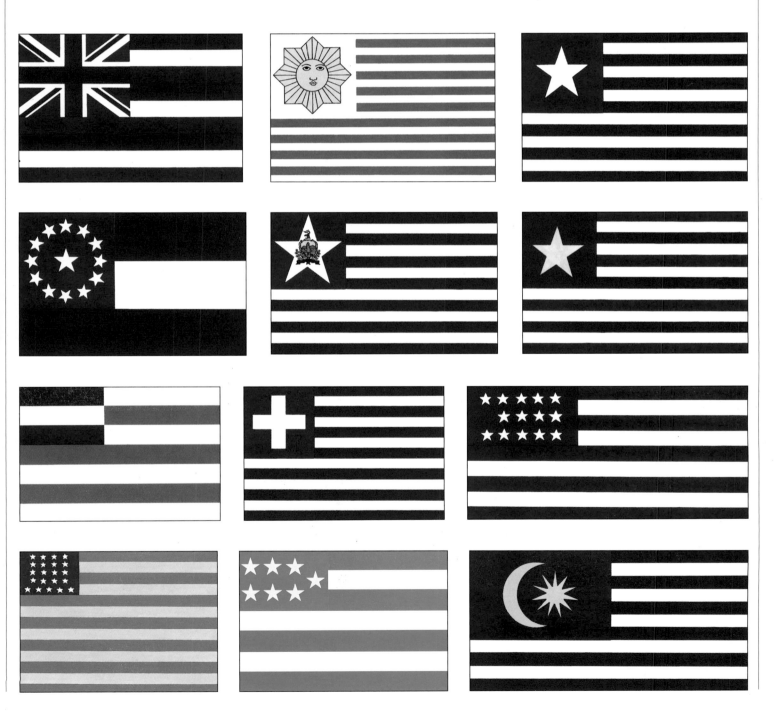

THE DUTCH AND PAN-SLAV COLOURS

Orange, white and blue were the livery colours of William I, Prince of Orange (1533–1584). Armbands in these colours were worn by his soldiers at the siege of Leiden in 1574, and in the 1580s they were used on the horizontal tricolour of the ensign and the flag used on land. Thus was created the first modern flag, displaying simple stripes instead of heraldic devices.

During the 17th century the orange was gradually replaced by red. This may have been because red is more visible at sea, or the reason may have been political: a manifestation of the Dutch estates-general's wish to exclude the House of Orange. The original tricolour survived until at least 1795, when the orange was officially replaced by red.

In the 18th century the Dutch ensign was one of a few that were well known in many parts of the world, especially South-east Asia, North America and South Africa. In South Africa seven political entities adopted flags based on the Dutch design: Natalia (1839), Transvaal (1857), Orange Free State (1857), Lyndenburg Republic (1857), Goshen Republic (1882), New Republic (1884) and the Union of South Africa (1928). In the Americas the original Dutch colours appear on the flag of New York, which is widely used in the city, while the modern colours (using red instead of orange) appear on the flag of the Netherlands Antilles.

The Dutch flag had an even greater impact on the flags of Slav nations in central and southern Europe. It was a model for the merchant flag of Russia, personally designed in 1699 by Tsar Peter the Great (1672–1725). Eager to modernize his country, he travelled incognito to western Europe in 1697 to gather first-hand information on advanced technology, especially in shipbuilding. He worked for four months as a shipwright in the shipyard of the Dutch East India Company in Zaandam, and

◆ **ABOVE**
Flag of the Netherlands (late 16th century–1795).

◆ **BELOW**
(from left to right)
Natal (1839–1843);
Transvaal (1857–1877);
Goshen Republic (1882–1885);
New Republic (1884–1888);
South Africa (1928–1994);
Netherlands Antilles (1959–1985).

THE FLAG FAMILY

The current national flags of the following countries belong to this family: BULGARIA, CROATIA, CZECH REPUBLIC, THE NETHERLANDS, THE NETHERLANDS ANTILLES, RUSSIA, SLOVAKIA, SLOVENIA, YUGOSLAVIA.

spent some time in the British Navy shipyard at Deptford. On his return to Russia he introduced an elaborate system of naval flags, based on Dutch and British flags and ensigns. The merchant flag, which became the national flag of Russia, was a horizontal tricolour of white-blue-red.

This flag, in turn, inspired other Slav countries to adopt horizontal tricolours displaying the same colours in different arrangements. Nations living under foreign (but not Russian) domination also followed suit. In 1835 the Serbs were the first to adopt a red-blue-white tricolour for their ships on inland waters. In 1848, during the first pan-Slav Congress in Prague, these were proclaimed the pan-Slav colours and were adopted of horizontal tricolours by several Slav provinces of Austria. The Slovaks and Slovenes placed the colours in the same order as Russia, the Serbs adopted a blue-red-white tricolour and the Croats

positioned the colours as in the Dutch flag. The flag adopted by Bulgaria in 1878 was the same as that of Russia, the only difference being the substitution of green for the red. In 1880 Montenegro adopted a merchant ensign, a tricolour similar to that of Serbia with a white cross in the centre of the red stripe. A year later the cross had been removed and a crown with the royal cipher "H.I", for Nikola I, placed in the centre. The Kingdom of Serbs, Croats and Slovenes, established in 1918, adopted a national flag and ensign in the form of a horizontal blue-white-red tricolour, which remained unchanged when the name of the country was changed to Yugoslavia.

A somewhat different flag belonging to this flag family is that of Czechoslovakia (currently the Czech Republic), adopted in 1920.

There are other flags that do not belong to this family, but are worth mentioning because their design (horizontal tricolour) is copied from that of the Russian flag. These are the flags and ensigns of nations that were once part of the Russian Empire and gained independence either temporarily or permanently: Belarus (1918–1919 and 1991–1995), some Cossack states, Lithuania, Estonia, Azerbaijan, Armenia, Uzbekistan and Tajikistan.

◆ **BELOW**
(from left to right)
Russia (c.1700–1858, 1883–1918, since 1991); Bulgaria (since 1878); Slovakia (1848); Montenegro (1881–1918); Serbia (1882–1918); Croatia (1941–1945).

THE FRENCH *TRICOLORE*

The colours red, blue and white have been successively used on French flags from the time of Charlemagne. Red was the imperial flag from the 9th century; blue was the field of the armorial banner of France from the 13th century to 1589, and of the merchant ensign from 1661 to 1790; and white was the French flag and ensign from 1589 to 1790. Nevertheless, it is surprisingly only a coincidence that these three colours appear together on the French national flag; they are, in fact, the colours of the coat of arms of the city of Paris, combined with the white of the Bourbons.

On 13 July 1789, on the eve of the French Revolution, the Paris militia were given blue and red cockades. Four days later in the City Hall the Marquis de Lafayette presented a similar cockade to King Louis XVI, who attached it to the royal white one. The leaders of the Revolution approved the Marquis' proposal to adopt the cockade in the "colours of liberty". The new cockade was received enthusiastically by the people and in the following days the streets of Paris were full of ribbons and flags in the "colours of liberty" in various arrangements.

In spite of this fervour, the official flag and ensign remained unchanged. The addition of a tricolour streamer to the war ensign in 1790 did not satisfy the rebellious sailors, who demanded the introduction of a new one displaying the colours that were already perceived as the national ones. The ensign that was subsequently adopted on 24 October 1790 was white with the canton composed of a red-white-blue vertical tricolour and a white border separating it from the outer border, which was half-red and half-blue. The vertical arrangement of three colours was revolutionary, both geometrically and politically. The order of colours was changed to the present one on 15 February 1794.

A few decades after the French Revolution the colours of the *Tricolore*, as the flag is called, were perceived in Europe and elsewhere as the

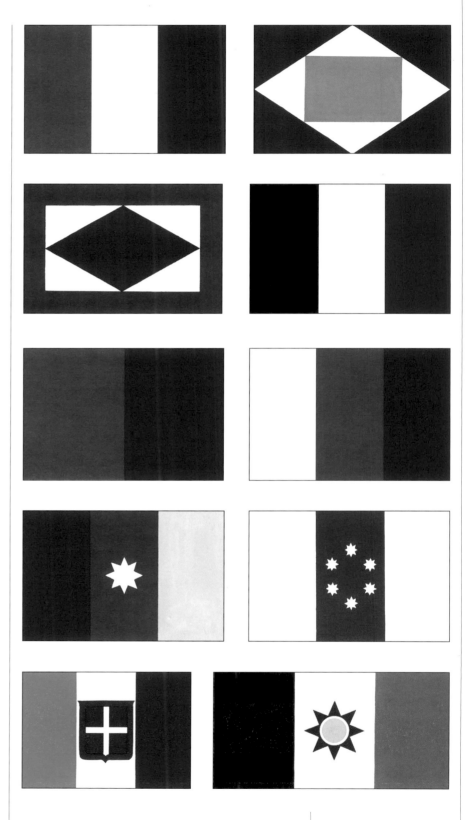

♦ **ABOVE**
(left to right from top left)
France (1794–1815 and since 1830); Italian Republic (1802–1805); Lucca (1803–1805); Rome Republic; Haiti (1804–1805); Mexico (1815–1821); Colombia, civil ensign (1834–1861); Ecuador, civil ensign (1845–1860); Italy, national flag and ensign (1848–1946); Iraq (1959–1963).

colours of the republican movement. They were adopted by Lucca (1803), Uruguay (1825–1828), the Dominican Republic (1844), Costa Rica (1848) and the Polish insurgents of 1863. Even more influential was the *Tricolore* design introduced by Napoleon in some Italian states. This later inspired revolutionaries and leaders of independence movements in many parts of the world to adopt flags with a vertical arrangement of colours. The first was the French colony of Saint Domingue where the revolutionaries had already in 1803 adopted a blue-red flag: the French flag without the white which they perceived as a symbol of their oppressors. On 1 January 1804 this became the first national flag of independent Haiti. Flags with three vertical stripes were adopted by revolutionary movements or governments in Mexico (1815), Belgium (1831), Colombia (1834), Ecuador (1845), Ireland (1848), Italy (1848) and Iraq (1958), and the King of Romania (1867).

A large group of flags with the French *Tricolore* in the canton are those of the French colonies created in the 19th and 20th centuries. When Saarland was part of the French occupation zone in Germany after World War II, the French authorities introduced a flag displaying the French colours.

The next large addition to the family of vertical tricolours came in the second half of the 20th century, when many former French colonies in Africa adopted flags following the *Tricolore* design.

THE FLAG FAMILY

The current national flags of the following countries belong to this family: ANDORRA, BELGIUM, CAMEROON, CHAD, FRANCE, GUINEA, IRELAND, ITALY, IVORY COAST, MALI, MEXICO, MOLDOVA, PERU, ROMANIA, RWANDA, SENEGAL, WALLIS AND FUTUNA.

FLAGS OF THE FRENCH COLONIES

TAHITI 1845–1880
RAIATEA 1880–1897
RIMATARA 1891–1900
LUANG PRABANG 1893–1947
LEBANON 1920–1943
LATAKIA 1922–1936
JABAL AD DURUZ 1922–1936
FRENCH MOROCCO 1923–1956
SYRIA 1925–1932
ANNAM 1930–1940
TOGO 1956–1960
GABON 1959–1960

THE LIVERY COLOURS

The simplest national flags, introduced by several European countries during the last two centuries, are those composed of livery colours arranged in two or three horizontal stripes. In most cases the upper stripe is in the colour of a heraldic charge, while the lower stripe displays the colour of the shield, although the reverse order of colours was customary in Austria. When translating coats of arms into flags, gold becomes yellow and silver becomes white. The only exception to this rule is the German flag, called *Schwarz-Rot-Gold* (black-red-gold), which has a golden yellow stripe instead of yellow.

From 1785 to 1931, and since 1936, the colours of the Spanish ensigns have been yellow and red, the armorial colours of Castile, Aragón, Catalonia and Navarre. The Spanish republican

colours (1931–1939) were red, yellow and purple (the colour of the lion in the arms of León). The flag of Portugal from 1821 to 1910 displayed livery colours dating from the 12th century. National flags in livery colours were most widespread in central Europe, especially in the German states and parts of Austria-Hungary. The colours of the proper arms of Austria (a white fess on red field) were

◆ ABOVE AND LEFT
(from left to right) Spain, civil ensign (1785–1928); Spain, civil ensign (1931–1939); Portugal (1821–1910); Württemberg (1816–1935); Brunswick (1748–1814); Saxony (1815–1935); Saxony-Weimar-Eisenach (1815–1920); Mecklenburg (1863–1935); Prussia, civil ensign (1823–1863); Germany 1867–1919.

◆ **RIGHT**
(from left to right)
Austria, national flag
(1804–1918);
Galicia and Lodomeria
(1849–1890);
Austria-Hungary, civil ensign
(1869–1918);
Romania (1861–1867);
Russia, national flag
(1858–1883;,
San Marino, national flag
(since 1862).

◆ **FAR RIGHT**
National flag of Bohemia
(1914–1918); Czechoslovakia
(1918–1920) and Poland
(since 1919).

employed on the civil ensign of 1869-1918 and thereafter on the national flag. The national flag of Austria, used from 1804 to 1918, displayed the colours of the imperial arms (a black double-headed eagle on a golden field). A few other examples are the flags or ensigns of Brunswick, Saxony, Saxony-Weimar-Eisenach, Württemberg, Prussia, Mecklenburg, Germany, Galicia and Lodomeria, Hungary and Austria-Hungary. The first flag of Romania displayed the livery colours of Valachia and Moldavia. For a short period the Russian national flag displayed the colours of the imperial arms (black double-headed eagle on a golden field) and white from the charge of the arms of Moscow. Other flags with livery colours are those of San Marino, Luxembourg, Monaco, the Vatican, Poland and Ukraine.

THE FLAG FAMILY

The national flags of the following countries belong to this family:

AUSTRIA, GERMANY, HUNGARY, LUXEMBOURG, MONACO, POLAND, SAN MARINO, SPAIN, UKRAINE, VATICAN.

THE PAN-ARAB COLOURS

The early Arab flags were of one colour, often charged with religious inscriptions. Biographers of the Prophet Muhammad ascribe to him two flags, one black and one white; his followers are said to have fought under the white flag for seven years and with this flag they entered Mecca. White was also the colour of the Muslim dynasty of the Umayyads, the immediate successors of the Prophet and an influential family of the Quraish tribe to which he belonged. Under a white flag the Umayyads ruled the Muslim Empire from AD 661 to 750, and were Muslim rulers of Spain from AD 756 to 1031. Black, the second colour used by Muhammad, was the colour of the Abbasid dynasty that overthrew the Umayyads and ruled the Muslim Empire from AD 750 to 1258.

Green, perceived as the colour of Islam, was the traditional colour of the Fatimid dynasty of caliphs, which ruled in North Africa from AD 909 to 1171. The Fatimids were leaders of the Ismaili sect and claimed descent from Fatima, the daughter of the Prophet Muhammad. Red is the colour of the Hashemites, descendants of Hashim, the great-grandfather of the Prophet Muhammad, and for centuries the hereditary amirs of Mecca. The founder of the modern Hashemite dynasty was Husayn ibn Ali, the amir of Mecca, King of Hejaz (1916–1924) and father of the kings of Iraq and Jordan.

In 1911 a group of young Arabs met in the Literary Club in Istanbul to choose a design for a modern Arab flag, and decided it should be composed of these four colours – white, black, green and red. The symbolism was explained by the poet Safi al-Din al-Hili:

White are our deeds, black are our battles,
Green are our fields, red are our knives.

In 1914 the central committee of the Young Arab Society in Beirut declared that the flag of the future independent Arab state should display the colours of the Umayyads (white), Abbasids (black) and Fatimids (green). However, the Arab Revolt began in Hejaz on 10 June 1916 under a

◆ **LEFT**
Hijaz (1917–1920).

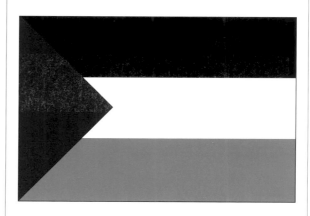

◆ **LEFT**
Hijaz (1920–1926) and Iraq (1921–1924).

◆ **LEFT**
Syria (1920).

plain red flag, traditional for that area. Several months later Sharif Hussein, leader of the revolt, accepted suggestions to adopt the colours white, black and green, and added red, a symbol of his family. The flag was hoisted on 30 May 1917,

THE FLAG FAMILY

The current national flags of the following countries and territories belong to this family:
EGYPT, IRAQ, JORDAN, KUWAIT, PALESTINE, SOMALILAND, SUDAN, SYRIA, UNITED ARAB EMIRATES, WESTERN SAHARA, YEMEN.

a day that might be considered the birthday of the pan-Arab colours.

The flag family started to grow when this modern Arab flag was adopted by Syria in March 1920 and by Iraq in 1921. By adding a white star (Syria) or two stars (Iraq) to the flag, both countries manifested that they were the first and second state to emanate from the "mother-state". The designs of these flags were later modified, but the four pan-Arab colours were retained and were adopted by Transjordan (1921), Palestine (1922), Kuwait (1961), the United Arab Emirates (1971), Western Sahara (1976) and Somaliland (1996).

After the revolution of 1952 in Egypt, the young officers who abolished the monarchy introduced the Arab Liberation Flag, a horizontal red-white-black tricolour, which symbolized the period of oppression (black) overcome through bloody struggle (red) to be replaced by a bright future (white). This flag was the inspiration for the flags of several Arab nations which chose the republican political system, so it could be considered to be the first of the second generation of pan-Arab colours. With the addition of two green stars (for Egypt and Syria), in 1958 it became the national flag of the United Arab Republic. Later similar flags, with or without stars, were adopted by Yemen (1962), Syria and Iraq (1963), South Yemen (1967), Libya (1969) and Sudan (1970).

◆ ABOVE
(left to right from top left)
Iraq (1924–1959);
Syria (1932–1958 and
1961–1963);
United Arab Republic
(1958–1961) and Egypt
(1961–1972);
Iraq (1963–1991) and Syria
(1963–1971);
Yemen (1962–1990);
Libya (1969–1972);
South Yemen (1967–1990).

THE PAN-AFRICAN COLOURS

Two factors have influenced the choice of colours for the flags of independent countries south of the Sahara. The first, and main, source of inspiration was the green, yellow and red flag of Ethiopia, the oldest independent state in Africa. The second was the red, black and green flag designed in 1917 by Marcus Garvey, the organizer of the first important black unification movement in the United States. He created the flag for the United Negro Improvement Association, but wanted it to become the national flag of a new unified black state he dreamt of creating. In 1957, Ghana became the

◆ **RIGHT**
(from top to bottom)
Mali Federation (1959–1961);
Biafra (1967–1970);
Cape Verde (1975–1992).

◆ **FAR LEFT**
The national flag of Ethiopia.

◆ **FAR LEFT**
Marcus Garvey's flag.

THE FLAG FAMILY

The current national flags of the following countries belong to this family:
ANGOLA, BENIN, BURKINA FASO, CAMEROON, CENTRAL AFRICAN REPUBLIC, CONGO, ETHIOPIA, GHANA, GUINEA, GUINEA-BISSAU, KENYA, MALAWI, MALI, MOZAMBIQUE, RWANDA, SÃO TOMÉ AND PRÍNCIPE, SENEGAL, SOUTH AFRICA, TOGO, UGANDA, ZAMBIA, ZIMBABWE.

first independent country in western Africa to adopt a flag in these colours. Its flag, in the Ethiopian colours with a black star, was inspired by the flag of the Black Star Line shipping company established by Garvey in Accra.

The Ethiopian colours and pan-Africanism ideas heralded by President Kwame Nkrumah influenced many other African leaders. Indeed, President Sékou Touré of Guinea's extensive description of the symbolic meaning of the red, yellow and green in 1958 helped to consolidate the conviction that these three colours may also be regarded as pan-African.

Ghana's example was followed by other African countries which adopted flags displaying the same colours: the Mali Federation (1959-1961), Rwanda (1961), Zambia (1964), Guinea Bissau (1973), São Tomé and Príncipe (1975), Cape Verde (1975-1992), Zimbabwe (1980), Mozambique (1983) and South Africa (1994).

The first country in Africa to adopt Garvey's colours as its main flag colours was Kenya in 1963, which was closely followed by Malawi in 1964 and Biafra in 1967. In all three flags the black stands for the people, the red symbolizes the blood shed in the struggle for independence, and the green represents the land with its fertile fields and forests.

The Ethiopian colours in various arrangements were adopted by Benin, Burkina Faso, Cameroon, Congo (Brazzaville) and Togo. Some other countries (Angola, Central African Republic, Namibia, Seychelles, Tanzania and Uganda) display on their flags three of the four pan-African colours.

Most of the flags displaying the pan-African colours are still in use.

◆ **RIGHT**
(left to right)
South Kasai (1960–1962);
Cameroon (1961–1975).

◆ **RIGHT**
Zanzibar (1963–1964).

◆ **RIGHT**
(left to right)
Burundi (1962–1966);
Zaire (1971–1997).

INDEX